# THE GOOD RULER

# ★ The
# ★ Good
# ★ Ruler

## From Herbert Hoover to
## Richard Nixon

# Bruce Kuklick

**Rutgers University Press**

**New Brunswick and London**

**Library of Congress Cataloging-in-Publication Data**
Kuklick, Bruce, 1941–
The good ruler: from Herbert Hoover to Richard Nixon / by Bruce
Kuklick.
p.  cm.
Bibliography: p.
Includes index.
ISBN 0-8135-1282-4
1. Presidents—United States—History—20th century.
2. Presidents—United States—Public opinion—History—20th century.
3. Public opinion—United States—History—20th century.  4. United
States—Politics and government—20th century.  I. Title.
E176.1.K84 1988
973.9'092'2—dc19                                     87-16026
                                                          CIP

British Cataloging-in-Publication Information Available

*For Marya*

# ★ Contents

# ★ List of Illustrations

# ★ Acknowledgments

I have presented many of the ideas in this book to various graduate and undergraduate classes, but I especially wish to thank the students in History 164 (formerly History 65b) at the University of Pennsylvania for helpful discussions over the last several years. The following people were all good enough to read early versions of the manuscript of this book: Lee Benson, Paul Dry, Richard Freeland, David Johnson, Edward Mannino, Murray Murphey, Richard Neustadt, Robert Schulzinger, and William Wolff. Elizabeth Block, Leo Ribuffo, and Marc Trachtenberg all read several versions of the book.

# THE GOOD RULER

The mind is its own place, and in itself
Can make a Heav'n of Hell, a Hell of Heav'n
John Milton, *Paradise Lost*

"I am Oz, the Great and Terrible," said the little
man, in a trembling voice, "but don't strike me—please
don't!—and I'll do anything you want me to."
Our friends looked at him in surprise and dis-
may. . . . "How can I help being a humbug," he said,
"when all these people make me do things that everybody
knows can't be done?"
Frank Baum, *The Wonderful Wizard of Oz*

# ★ Preface

The study of American political history from the Great Depression to Watergate has emphasized the issues and the programs of national leadership. Historians regularly engage in ranking and grading the achievements of the presidents. Nonetheless, scholars radically disagree and repeatedly fail to reach a consensus about the meaning of issues and about the goodness or badness of policies, and consequently on the grades that presidents should get. This failure is most pointedly illustrated in the conflicting nature of what I call the "would have" statements that appear in the analyses of historians.

The best example is the case of John Kennedy. Kennedy's defenders say if he had lived, the United States would not have fought in Vietnam; and so, on this view, JFK's stature is enhanced. In contrast, his critics urge that, like Lyndon Johnson, Kennedy's reputation would have been stained by the immorality of the war; and so, on this contradictory view, Kennedy's stature is diminished. Historians think they can justify "would have" propositions and thus make evaluations that will command assent. But their continual disputes are evidence that such evaluations are elusive.

In this book I have examined the difficulties of historians concerned with issues by pointing out conflicts over "would have" statements; and I have argued that we cannot make sense of what "would have" happened had events been otherwise than they were.

In place of policy-oriented histories, with their range of explicit and implicit "would have' statements, I have substituted an approach that gives primacy not to issues but to the collective passions of the people. This story formally begins with chapter 1, The Inspirational Presidency. To put the reader in an appropriate frame of mind, however, the introduction obliquely attacks our conventional ways of looking at political history. This introduction presents a fable to suggest how "would have" statements mold our ideas.

# ★ Introductory Fable: What If?

**R**ichard Nixon's electoral victory in 1960 was the closest in American political history, the triumph perhaps tarnished by voting irregularities in crucial states that went Republican by narrow margins. Nonetheless, in a secret agreement that only came to light later, an aide to John Kennedy—Nixon's defeated opponent—met with Nixon and suggested that Kennedy would not dispute Nixon's claims if Kennedy could choose the secretaries of state and treasury. Later critics have argued that Nixon should never have acquiesced in what, from the records of the conference, appears to be a threat of blackmail on the part of the Democrats. Nixon's associates have argued, however, that he faced a terrible dilemma. The evidence now demonstrates that electoral irregularities on the Democratic side were greater than those of the GOP. Nixon, indeed, had won the election and could have won a fight over its outcome. But for Nixon to have dismissed the Kennedy offer, the argument goes, would have risked a constitutional crisis and the electorate's faith in the political process itself. In this unfortunate situation, some historians contend, Nixon allowed Kennedy the choice of the two cabinet positions. This positive analysis is borne out by

*1. Richard Nixon and Henry Cabot Lodge*

Democratic documents indicating that the Kennedy men were willing to risk a public confrontation with Nixon, despite having a flimsy case.

In due course, in what has been called "the compromise of 1960," Nixon appointed Adlai Stevenson as secretary of the treasury and prominent Texas Democrat John Connally as secretary of state. Kennedy calculated that these appointments would solidify his control over both the eastern and southern wings of his party, strengthening the bid he planned, even then, for another try at the presidency in 1964. Kennedy also reasoned that the Stevenson-Connally presence in the cabinet would be strong enough to enable the Democrats to get some credit for any GOP accomplishments, yet weak enough for them to avoid being blamed for any GOP mistakes.

Kennedy's strategy seemed initially to work, when the Stevenson appointment enraged Republican conservatives and underscored the potency of liberal Democrats. Yet Nixon's cautious policies at home and abroad soon reassured the GOP. The president quickly came to stand for a continuation of Eisenhower Republicanism but could also point to the bipartisan nature of his cabinet to argue for the consensual nature of his presidency. The support he may have lost with the GOP right was more than balanced by the inroads he made with moderate Democrats. Nixon safeguarded American business interests, refused to expand the welfare system, and conducted a prudent yet firm anticommunist foreign policy.

At the same time Nixon's first-term policies were different from Eisenhower's. He was some twenty-five years younger than Ike, and there was a new youthful tone to the White House. With the exception of Teddy Roosevelt, RMN was the youngest elected president, "born in this century," as he put it. He had two attractive daughters, and they and his wife Pat set the style for a new cultural look. Nixon himself contributed by a self-conscious attempt to express the intellectual tempo of the sixties. Philosopher-longshoreman Eric Hoffer, author of the famed *True Believer,* conducted seminars on democratic and totalitarian politics for the presidential coterie. Movie star Gregory Peck did readings from the great works of American literature at the White House, and Montovani presented a series of string "American musicales." In the most celebrated event, before a glittering Washington audience, Arthur Miller directed an original one-act drama featuring Marilyn Monroe.

Historians have acknowledged that the achievements of the first administration were more apparent than real. But there was also a genuine shift in the spirit of the people during the early days of Nixon's "New Frontier." The president's "coalition of the reasonable" made it patent that the ship of state was on a steady course. The president reinvigorated his office after the doldrums of Eisenhower's last two years, yet he also provided the solid stability the people wanted.

Of course, as historians have also acknowledged, Nixon's real achievements came in his second term, when foreign policy dominated American life.

Eisenhower had begun to send United States advisers to shore up the weak South Vietnamese government threatened by the external aggression of the North. Nixon continued this policy and quietly escalated aid to the beleaguered southerners. The president did not want war but was determined that communism should not gain a victory. RMN had in mind the problems of Korea: he knew the political liabilities of fighting a limited war to repel aggression, yet he also recognized the imperative need to do so.

In November 1963 the situation in South Vietnam worsened when President Diem was assassinated by subversives. The nation-building in Southeast Asia to which the administration was committed suffered a severe setback, and for the next several months Nixon searched for a coherent policy. Although it was not apparent to the public in the early part of 1964, South Vietnam was on the verge of collapse. The president turned things around in his famous television speech of June 15, 1964. Flanked by former President Eisenhower, with whom Nixon had consulted at length, Secretary of State Connally, and Secretary of Defense William Knowland, Nixon declared a national emergency and asked for mobilization of the armed forces to roll back Asian communism and secure "a generation of peace." He asked Congress for a declaration of war against North Vietnam, and called immediately for the deployment of 150,000 troops, with further increases to 650,000 by the end of the year.

Overall, the nation responded well. Some friendly critics have urged that a more gradual escalation of the war would have promoted greater consensus and cut the ground from under professional Nixon-baiters. The Nixon-baiters have contended that the timing of the speech was political—a move designed to secure the president's reelection. But available records show otherwise: events in South Vietnam were moving rapidly, and Nixon had to decide sometime between April and July whether the United States ought to commit itself or retreat in Asia. Moreover, although the war footing on which RMN placed the country was unpopular with some groups, most commentators have conceded that Nixon showed great courage in not following a path of retreat. It is at least true, however, that the president used Eisenhower's great prestige to gain support for the administration's policies. Nixon cultivated Eisenhower and went out of his way to identify himself with the general. Ike did not like being used by Nixon, and in foreign affairs he had always moved slowly. At the same time Eisenhower was fully behind Nixon's policies. As he said the day after Nixon's speech: "We must not surrender South Vietnam to communism"; once we "put our prestige on the line we must hit them with everything necessary for victory."

Nixon was also served well by his "Kennedy appointees," who gave him a war cabinet that represented the major interests of both parties. Of the three cabinet members responsible for running the war—Connally, Stevenson, and Knowland—two were Democrats. Connally agreed with the effort, and consolidated the support of Democrats like Senators "Scoop" Jackson and Lyndon Johnson. Stevenson at Treasury was a reluctant advocate, and Nixon eased him out of the cabinet when the war was effectively won in 1966. Nonetheless, Stevenson did not make his complaints public and did an admirable technical job of preventing the economy from overheating during the fighting. His high reputation as the conflict's "financial wizard" was only marginally damaged (after his death in 1968) by the revelation that he had been a weak and defeatist voice in the Nixon White House.

Although historians have disagreed on the exact goals Nixon had in mind in declaring war, they have agreed that the president took a risky step. He seemed to realize this himself when he said he would rather be a "one-term president" than have the United States yield to communism. Despite public support for mobilization, it was not until a series of battlefield victories in early October 1964 that Nixon went ahead of his opponent in the campaign, Hubert Humphrey, and scored a decisive victory in the November election.

Kennedy's calculations had been as shrewd as Nixon's. Reckoning that the voters would not turn out an incumbent during a war, Kennedy privately began to reassess his announced candidacy after Nixon's June speech. Previously the frontrunner for his party's nomination, Kennedy concluded by the end of June that no Democrat could win. The question for him was: how could he gracefully withdraw from the candidacy without damaging his credit with the party for a possible run in 1968?

The answer came in early July when Kennedy's brother Robert, a prominent congressman from Massachusetts, died in a tragic plane crash, leaving a grief-stricken wife and six children. Shortly thereafter, John Kennedy announced that his "family obligations" were "so overwhelming" that "he would not seek the nomination of his party for the presidency of the United States." When Kennedy dropped out of the race, only the liberal wing of the party had the ability to promote a candidate, and Humphrey easily took the nomination. But he was no match for a Republican who so easily commanded the right as well as the center. Kennedy's craft had paid off.

Nixon's second administration focused on the politics of war. The troop build-up went more slowly than expected, and the reform of the South Vietnamese government was fraught with bureaucratic troubles. Because the Americans initially suffered from weak generalship, it looked as if the president had mired the nation in a costly and useless struggle. Nixon's problems were increased by the utter intransigeance of the enemy. Throughout 1965 the North Vietnamese leader, Ho Chi Minh, refused to negotiate: all of Vietnam, he said, would fall under the sway of his communist government; all political forces in the country would be subject to his party's discipline; there could be no acceptance of counterrevolutionary elements. The year 1965 was also trying for Nixon as critics of the right and left, respectively, attacked his policies as either too dovish or too hawkish, as the language of the time had it.

At the beginning of 1966, however, Nixon's dilemmas were resolved by Ho himself, whom Walter LaFeber, the dean of American diplomatic historians, rightly called "the Hitler of Southeast Asia." In his crucial speech of early January 1966, Ho denounced the "lackeys of the American imperialists in South Vietnam," who would be "crushed" by the North because America was a "paper tiger."

Nixon had hitherto proceeded circumspectly. American troops fought only in the south, and the U.S. Air Force was not permitted to operate in the north. North Vietnamese troops had also, prior to Ho's speech, abided by informal constraints. Although there was large-scale infiltration into the south, the North Vietnamese regulars fought as guerillas and rarely engaged in wide, division-size encounters, preferring hit-and-run tactics. But shortly after Ho's speech, in what was called the "Tet Offensive," North Vietnamese regulars who had infiltrated south attacked in large units, inflicting a major defeat on American forces in Quang Tri, the northernmost city of the south.

Nixon responded with fortitude. He flew to Quang Tri to inspect the defeated troops and announced that the United States could no longer react like "a pitiful, helpless giant." He appointed a new and aggressive military commander—William Westmoreland—to carry the fight to the north to retaliate against the "reckless provocation." At home, meeting in extraordinary session, the Congress jointly and unanimously gave its "full and firm blessing" for the president to take whatever steps necessary to gain victory. The "Quang Tri Resolution"—formally the Resolution to the President in Respect to the Fighting at Quang Tri—gave Nixon a major boost. Not only did it commend the president's policies in the highest possible terms, but it also called upon the nation to rally around its leader.

Simultaneously with his speech at Quang Tri, Nixon had dispatched Secretary of Defense Knowland to Russia and Secretary of State Connally to Communist China. Each of these secret missions had the single aim of informing Moscow and Beijing that the United States would no longer tolerate the adventurist policies of North Vietnam. The Nixon administration wished it conveyed to the North Vietnamese that if there were not "in the very near future . . . clear signs of a willingness to negotiate," the United States would take "whatever measures were necessary to end the fighting." Knowland and Connally were specifically instructed to inform the Soviet and Chinese leadership that "no weapons were being excluded from consideration."

Four days after the return of the diplomats—on February 12, 1966—Ho repeated his attack on America as a "paper tiger" and called on the United States to surrender after its "Tet defeat." Nixon again dispatched Knowland and Connally. This time, however, they reported to Moscow and Beijing that in a week the United States would take military measures to end the war; but they added that America had no desire to topple the northern regime, only to maintain the territorial integrity of the South.

On February 19, 1966, a visibly shaken Nixon appeared on television to announce that the United States had dropped four tactical nuclear weapons in Vietnam. The first had been used against North Vietnamese regulars in "the second battle of Quang Tri." The president was able to report there the surrender of North Vietnamese

General Giap and the troops under his command. The other three weapons had been dropped on military and industrial installations near the North Vietnamese capital of Hanoi.

Nixon's decisions prompted the "February nuclear crisis." At the end of his speech the president had threatened continued nuclear bombing until the enemy should surrender its interest in the South. But he reiterated, this time in public, that the United States did not intend to overturn the northern regime; the American goal was only "the restoration of stability and tranquility in the south." Finally, RMN concluded, "these weapons of wrath" were "a last resort," used "in sorrow and not in anger." The United States hoped to be able to use its resources "pacifically and constructively to rebuild a new order of harmony and prosperity in Asia."

In retrospect it seems clear that the communist leadership in Hanoi, Moscow, and Beijing focused on the conciliatory aspects of Nixon's speech and the limited nature of the bombing. But at the time these dimensions of the president's strategy were not noted by many critics. Extremists, on the one hand, denounced RMN's assertion that the United States should only restore the *status quo ante bellum;* on the other hand, they demonstrated across the country because Nixon had used nuclear weapons.

The great mass of the public, however, backed the administration's deeds. At the same time, the people waited in deadly fear that China or the USSR might retaliate with nuclear weapons in Vietnam, or in the United States. For seventy-two hours during the crisis, the public was terrified that Nixon might have taken the first steps in the destruction of the planet, while simultaneously accepting the necessity for these steps.

On February 22 the president again addressed the nation, this time visibly relieved. Ho Chi Minh had declared that the war of liberation would stop, the president said. Nixon was also able to state that a ceasefire was occurring throughout Vietnam and that North Vietnamese troops were withdrawing behind the 1954 Geneva line.

Spending little time stressing the diplomatic victory, the bulk of Nixon's "President's Day Speech" outlined what came to be known as "the Nixon Plan": RMN proposed that all the nations of Southeast Asia—Laos, Cambodia, Thailand, North and South Vietnam, and the two Chinas—come together and formulate a program for regional economic and social development. The United States would lend "the helping hand of a friend" and "sustained material support" to this endeavor. The model for the Nixon Plan was, of course, the famous Marshall Plan of the late 1940s, and according to the documents, Nixon contemplated spending over $50 billion in Asian regional development.

The next months were busy ones for the president. The war wound down quickly in South Vietnam, but Nixon also supervised negotiations that ended much smaller though nasty conflicts in Laos and Cambodia. In these countries the United States accepted neutral regimes, overruling old antagonisms between reactionary and revolutionary factions. Connally's trip to China, in particular, had taken place in greatest secrecy, and as the Nixon Plan took shape, RMN himself made a widely praised trip to China—presaging diplomatic recognition. A few months later, in December 1966, Nixon traveled to the USSR to try to convince the Soviets that "the new era of peace in the Far East" did not mean that the United States would try to draw the nations of Asia into an alliance against the Russians. The president steadfastly refused to threaten the Soviets. Instead, he emphasized repeatedly that although the United States would not tolerate the subversive expansion of communism, this nation would also make a positive contribution to global stability and cooperation. The United States, Nixon said, had played "an imperative if unfortunate" role in "disturbing the material fabric of Asian society to protect its spiritual welfare";

now America would help those societies materially. Such aid would not be directed *against* any nation. "Specifically," said RMN, "we want the great Soviet people to ask its leadership to join with us in a constructive union." Featuring the speech on its front pages, *Pravda* praised it as the greatest statement by a Western politician since the time of FDR.

Because foreign policy dominated Nixon's second term, historians have not stressed as they should RMN's role in what has been called "the invisible revolution" of civil rights. This revolution culminated in the Civil Rights Acts of 1965 and 1966 that guaranteed voting rights and legal equality for black Americans in the south.

In 1957 Eisenhower had sent troops into Arkansas to bring about desegregation, and Nixon himself had always been committed to enforcing the law of the land. Some critics have charged that compelling the south to desegregate and to permit black voting was merely political on Nixon's part: he would attract black voters in the south and lose none of its white vote, irrevocably Democratic in any event. Other critics have added that an additional political consideration was the chance for the GOP to make inroads into the constituencies of liberal Democrats in the north. All of these criticisms overlook Nixon's sincere belief in the *petit bourgeois* ethic that he felt had made America great. He was admittedly opposed—vocally—to compelling social integration, as more doctrinaire supporters of black equality pointed out; and this opposition, it is true, enabled Nixon to secure the support of many blue-collar workers in the north as well as that of moderate southerners. Again, critics charged that Nixon's position was entirely political. But, on the other side, Nixon was four-square in pushing for legal equality and voting rights, "privileges," he said, "essential to any democratic society." Moreover, the president's critics ignored that he poured billions of dollars into his "black capitalist" projects in the north. Working hand in hand with Adam Clayton Powell, who became a revered black leader, Nixon again demonstrated his concern for a social order in which, as he put it, "everyone has the same chance at the starting gate."

The November 1966 elections were a great triumph for Nixon, the man. The president asked his countrymen not to vote by party but to vote for policies they approved, and the voters returned "Nixon Republicans" by the score. In the House, 304 Republicans were pitted against 127 Democrats; in the Senate the GOP had a 66–33 advantage; and state legislatures were overwhelmingly Republican. The first act of the 1967–68 Congress was to pass a bill requesting these legislatures to repeal the twenty-second amendment. The GOP eagerly hoped that RMN would run for a third term, as the repeal movement became a mighty tide in early 1967.

It is hard to believe that a political warrior like Nixon, still occasionally displaying the insecurity that had been so marked in the forties and fifties, could have resisted a chance for a third term. In March of 1967, however, the president was still unwilling to discuss his political future with even his closest associates, although some evidence indicates that his late March trip to southern California and his alma mater, Whittier College, was designed to be a first campaign round.

The trip ended in tragedy, when a psychologically disturbed student, enraged by Nixon's use of nuclear bombs, shot and killed the president. It is impossible to recapture the shock and despair of that bitter spring. "More than a president is dead," went a poet's lament, "And not ten thousand bullets in ten thousand heads could make the moment different." Few who were alive at the time will forget Nixon's stricken widow, her dress still bloody from cradling her husband's head, or a white and pale-faced Henry Cabot Lodge being sworn in as thirty-sixth president of the United States. Nixon's televized funeral was the greatest simultaneous communal experience in the history of the human race.

Lodge was a good and decent man, but he was not a mass leader. It seemed, too, as if all the fight had been taken out of the public. "We'll never be young again," said one of Nixon's aides. Stuffy, personally conservative, and without much popular presence, Lodge embodied a moribund eastern establishment. He tried in his famous "Let us continue" speech to carry on the momentum established by his predecessor, and he also made a gallant effort, soon after the funeral, to reaffirm Nixon's foreign policy by his trip to China, to initiate diplomatic recognition, and to Russia, to reassure the Soviets that he stood behind the policy of a constructive Asian union. But momentum *had* been lost, and Lodge was not leader enough to prevent a certain weariness and pessimism from gripping the electorate. By the fall of 1967 commentators were already expressing their sense of sadness by enunciating the terrible hypothetical that was so much a refrain of the next several years: "If only Nixon had lived."

The Nixon Plan hardly had a chance to take hold when the other grim event of the period occurred—the assassination of Lodge. The new president, former Speaker of the House Gerald Ford, took office in February 1968; he too was a decent man but of limited ability and, in 1968 at least, he was not fit to be president. In some ways he recognized this limitation when he tried to turn it to his advantage in his first major address by asserting "I'm a Ford, not a Lincoln."

There was inevitably a confusion of purpose as the lack of expertise of Ford and his staff became rapidly apparent. To this was added the public's predictable and understandable confusion of spirit in a difficult time. Worst of all, as soon as Ford got into office, he began to plot his election in November. Almost every politician would have succumbed to this lure, but Ford's campaigning at the ex-

pense of managing the government resulted in further
policy slippage.

Again Kennedy calculated shrewdly. After the death
of Nixon, he told his inner circle that no one could beat
Lodge. "Lodge," Kennedy said, "will win, but the vote will
be for Nixon. It's a no-win situation for the Democrats."
To the press he said, "I will not be a candidate in 1968."
Then, when Ford took over, Kennedy changed his mind.
Lodge was acceptable if gray. But, Kennedy believed, the
public had had too much. "They don't want unelected Republicans." After a suitable time mourning the dead president, Kennedy reappraised his position in the early spring
of 1968. He told reporters that the nation needed "sober
statesmanship" to carry it through "a painful period of
readjustment." He believed he could offer that leadership
to "a wounded nation."

Kennedy nailed down his nomination by securing the
services of Connally as his running mate. The Texan had
remained as secretary of state under Lodge and agreed to
stick it out under Ford. Not without ambition himself, the
secretary briefly thought of running as a Republican
against Ford in the primaries, but his Democratic credentials made him an unlikely candidate, and Ford himself was
determined to run. At best, on the GOP ticket, Connally
could hope to be Ford's vice president. On the other side,
although his reputation as Nixon's secretary of state was
great, he had become too closely identified with the Republicans to stand as the Democratic candidate. Kennedy
made him an offer he could not refuse: run for vice president as a Democrat and win; or as a Republican and lose.
Connally agreed with Kennedy's assessment of Ford's
chances, and in June—after barely concealed infighting
within the administration—Connally resigned as secretary
of state; and Kennedy announced that if he were nominated, he would ask Connally to run with him.

In November Kennedy won a convincing victory and,

given the choice, the voters made a wise decision, however wrong-headed subsequent events might make that judgment appear. At the very least, Kennedy was a major figure with substantial experience and a national constituency. In the next four years even grudging critics admit that he brought a measure of stability to the nation's highest office.

At the same time Kennedy's triumphs were largely without substance. To be sure, a lack of sustained achievement may also have characterized the first Nixon administration, but behind Nixon's words were deeds. Kennedy was enamored of Nixon's style, and consciously tried to emulate it. There was, however, little to back up the oratory—awkward phrasemaking in the style of the New Frontier, haunted by a second-hand quality.

In domestic affairs Kennedy offered a rehash of Congressional liberal measures that had been defeated in the early 1960s. Without an overpowering liberal coalition, they were again defeated in 1969 and 1970. In foreign affairs Vice President Connally—unofficial secretary of state and defense—brought a degree of competence, most notably in the neutralization of Cuba, which had been divided by communist and anticommunist factions. The president, however, overrode Connally's inclination to carry forward Nixon's assertive policies in the Far East. There, under Nixon, economic and social reconstruction would have proceeded apace, backed by military might. Kennedy lacked the determination, the "guts," Connally said privately, for such a task. The president wanted to avoid the appearance of defeat but seemed to care less about defeat itself. He effectively substituted for the Nixon Plan—now renamed "The Alliance for Progress"—"The Peace Corps," a much less costly but more gimmicky policy. Under its aegis young Americans were sent to Asia to do good works. There was much hoopla about the idealistic venture, but when it was terminated by Carter the results were inconsequential.

Connally was easily the strongest member of Kennedy's "team," to use the athletic language of the late sixties, but for that very reason he was a threat to Kennedy's leadership. The records show that the president began thinking soon after the inauguration about how to weaken Connally's position. Kennedy succeeded in 1972, because in June of that year Connally announced that he "would not serve in the next administration of our great leader."

Connally presents a fascinating study in American political life. Nixon aside, Connally was the most distinguished American statesman of the decade. For twelve years he guided the foreign policy of the United States, and from 1967 to 1972 was the essential force that prevented the disasters that befell America abroad thereafter; he was the most significant vice president the United States has had. Nonetheless, despite his own insight about America's long-term interests abroad and his concern for strength—economic, social, and military—in maintaining world order, he was unable to secure his own position. Three times Connally was used for Kennedy's ends: in 1960 when he became secretary of state, in 1968 when he became vice president, and in 1972 when he was refused renomination as vice president.

Had Connally not been burdened with strength as both a Republican and a Democratic, and therefore with liabilities in each party, he perhaps might have run for the presidency in 1976. For when accusations of misconduct prematurely ended the second Kennedy administration, Connally was the one significant associate of Kennedy's who was not in some way or other tarnished.

Four separate but connected series of happenings defined the Kennedy scandals. On assuming office he had appointed his younger brother, Edward, as attorney general. Edward Kennedy was a beefy, venal, political fixer whose taste for women and liquor had given him an unsavory reputation even in his home state of Massachusetts, where he presided over its congressional delegation. He was the same sort of flawed politician as his brother, except that he lacked the president's charm and finesse. Edward Kennedy's qualifications for the office of attorney general were slim, but he became his brother's most trusted adviser. As the policies of the administration abroad fragmented and Kennedy was unable to control his popularity at home, the president turned to Edward not so much for advice on policy as for suggestions about how to continue to control the White House regardless of achievement. The attorney general intimated that the investigative arm of the Justice Department might harass and intimidate political opponents. Thereafter, in 1971 and 1972, the Justice Department engaged in a plethora of "dirty tricks." The point was, for example, to occupy hostile journalists with the trouble of serious tax audits, so that, as Edward Kennedy said, they would "be put out of commission" as the president geared up for his reelection campaign. These "dirty tricks" comprised the first scandal.

The second scandal was Kennedy's collaboration with Senate majority leader Lyndon Johnson of Texas to extract large contributions from southwestern oil men and industrialists. At the president's suggestion, Johnson hinted to many prospective wealthy donors that legislation favorable to oil and gas interests would have "smooth sailing" if the president could be guaranteed election again.

The third scandal concerned Kennedy's appointment of Abe Fortas as chief justice of the Supreme Court in 1970, after his appointment as associate justice in 1969. In the hearings held on the former appointment, questions were raised about Fortas's relations with the president at that time. Fortas repeatedly denied that he and the president had consulted over the nation's political problems. It was later revealed, however, that from the time of his appointment in 1969 Fortas had regularly met with Kennedy to discuss issues the administration faced, and on many occasions had given the president his sense of how the

Supreme Court might rule on various cases, as well as how the court might be influenced. At the very least, these discussions were a grave breach of ethics, and before the judiciary committee, Fortas had perjured himself some dozen times by denying these discussions.

All of these unfortunate circumstances only came to light in the context of the intense inspection to which the inner workings of the administration were subject after its attempt to "cover up" Edward Kennedy's involvement in the death of Mary Jo Kopechne on Chappaquiddick Island off Martha's Vineyard on Labor Day weekend of 1972. The events surrounding this last scandal are still unclear. Edward Kennedy and some cronies spent a weekend, they said, entertaining some female members of their staffs, including Kopechne, one of the late Robert Kennedy's female aides. A car apparently driven by Kennedy but also containing the young woman ended up in the bottom of the channel between the Vineyard and the island. She died, while the attorney general escaped. But he failed to report the "accident," and his complicity in her death was at first unknown.

Faced with a serious challenge to his campaign for reelection, the president went on television and asserted his complete faith in his brother's innocence. The president said, however, that the public should have no doubts about the integrity of its system of justice. He suspended his brother "without prejudice" until such time as an extraordinary "High Judicial Commission" should report on the case. To head this commission, he appointed Chief Justice Abe Fortas; the Justice Department was placed in the hands of an old Kennedy intimate, Deputy Attorney General Archibald Cox. Cox was "to make all the resources of the Department immediately and unstintingly available" to Fortas for the prosecution of the case. At the same time, as White House tapes later revealed, the president instructed Fortas and Cox, first, at least "to keep a lid on matters" until after the election; and, second, "before if possible, later if necessary" to exonerate his brother.

In mid-October 1972—three weeks before the election—the "Fortas Report" got both Kennedys off the hook, or at least so most historians have concluded. It must be added, however, that the voting patterns do not prove that the narrow victory Kennedy won against Nelson Rockefeller was much affected by the report.

Even in the last month of the campaign there were politically inspired attacks on the "objectivity" of the report, but not until two months later, at the time of the second inaugural, did such concern become public and widespread.

The "unravelling" of what became known as "the Chappaquiddick scandals" was mainly the work of Edward Kennedy's alcoholic wife, Joan. Joan Kennedy, in various stages of coherence at various times, talked to investigative journalists and Republican politicians, putting them on the trail of Fortas and of corrupt practices in the Justice Department.

By the spring of 1973 the select committee of Senator Sam Ervin, Democrat of North Carolina, began its televised hearings, and the president was forced to appoint a special prosecutor with no ties to his entourage. Although politically motivated, Special Prosecutor John Mitchell, an important New York lawyer, was scrupulously fair as well as unrelenting, as was his successor Richard Kleindienst, who had been attorney general in the Nixon administration. In September Edward Kennedy's trial began in a Massachusetts court on a charge of manslaughter. The front-page headlines about the trial had to compete with equally disturbing news about corruption in the administration.

In October and November the Kennedy regime began to fall. Edward Kennedy had briefly returned to his post as attorney general but he resigned in April, his place taken by Cox. In October Cox resigned, as did Chief Justice

Fortas. In early November Senator Johnson traded his resignation for a jail sentence: the Senate majority leader, investigation proved, had taken bribes that had not been reported as income; because he left his position in the Senate, he would not be tried for income tax evasion.

On November 22, 1973, the president himself stepped down. His party was in tatters, his popularity hovered at 20 percent, and criminal charges were pending. Nonetheless, Kennedy denied all wrongdoing. He left the presidency, he said, because "partisan pressure" had made it impossible for him to function adequately. However unjust these pressures were, the president added, they were "undermining the presidential office itself." He left the White House after a tearful speech about his family's contribution to American public life, a contribution, he said, that had begun with his father. "My father was a saint," he cried, as he walked from the Oval Office.

Even in the short run, historians have observed that the significance of the scandals was inflated at the time as a great fear of conspiracy swept the nation. Evidence at our disposal now, for example, demonstrates that even Nixon secretly taped White House conversations and used his powers during the war to monitor and control opponents of his policies. Moreover, Kennedy's later rehabilitation as an elder statesman testifies to the ability of the public to forgive and forget. Finally, in February 1974, Edward Kennedy was found "not guilty" and discharged; even hostile critics acknowledge that his real guilt consisted primarily in a dubious personal morality and weakness of character, not criminal negligence or intent. The president initiated "the Chappaquiddick cover-up" to cover up nothing.

On the other hand, it was the president's willingness to break the law if it was necessary that constituted the "breach of faith," as Theodore White put it, for which he was rightly driven from office.

In light of the events of 1972–73, the rest of Kennedy's career took on a sinister hue, as was made clear in Arthur Schlesinger's acutely sensitive memoir, *The Imperial Presidency*. Schlesinger was a speechwriter and intellectual in residence in the Kennedy White House. Although he was utterly reliable, Kennedy thought him a political naif. When the outlines of the cover-up began to take shape in September of 1972, Kennedy asked Schlesinger "to coordinate for the Chief Justice the various aspects of the investigation of his brother." But as Kennedy put it to the attorney general, if there were any unfortunate repercussions, Schlesinger would "take the fall" and "be left dangling, dangling in the wind." Kennedy never resorted to this strategy, as Schlesinger emphasized in his book, although "the plan" accounts for some of Schlesinger's bitterly extreme claims.

Schlesinger argues that the compromise of 1960 (which became public during the unravelling of the cover-up); the decision not to run in 1964 and to run in 1968; and the refusal to continue Nixon's policies in the Far East—all point to a similar absence of principle. Kennedy, says Schlesinger, "went out as he came in"; he had "no class." Schlesinger, too, expressed the oft-repeated lament: if only Nixon had lived. . . .

At the 1972 Democratic Convention that had formally dumped Connally, Kennedy selected James Carter, governor of Georgia, as his running mate. Carter was a newcomer to politics, and was easily controlled by Kennedy. But, like Connally, he was a southerner and brought a conventional balance to the ticket. He was also young, personally appealing, and honest—easing the fears of people who were suspicious of the image of political operatives that surrounded Kennedy. Ten months after he took the oath as vice president, Carter was president. His national experience was drastically limited and he limped to the end of Kennedy's term.

Kennedy's foreign policy, high-flown in rhetoric, was

short on will, and the consequences though long in coming were clear when they arrived. The détente characterizing the last two years of the Nixon presidency waned under Kennedy as tensions grew between the United States and the USSR. Under the inexperienced Carter—without the steadying hand of a Connally—things got worse. War broke out between the left and right in Laos and Cambodia. Moreover, Kennedy had also failed to stem the internal decay of the South Vietnamese regime that Nixon had resurrected. This development, it is true, had begun under Lodge and Ford, as the shifts in the American government made American policy incoherent and heartened subversive elements. Under Kennedy, however, the communists saw new evidence that the United States was indeed a "paper tiger," as the president's grandiloquence—we shall "pay any price, bear any burden"—was conclusively falsified by Kennedy's unwillingness to act.

Under the post-Nixon Republicans and then later under Kennedy, the public was unaware of the weakness of the American response to renewed subversion. Under Carter the delicate structure of peace in the Far East crumbled as the whole of Southeast Asia became a tinderbox of revolution.

By 1976 the GOP believed that it had a virtual mandate to the White House—manifest foreign policy failures under Carter and the domestic taint of Chappaquiddick gave license to all Republican presidential hopefuls. Ronald Reagan and Barry Goldwater, "the two old men of the right," initially contested delegates. But these delegates were split between the two; more important, Nixon's reign had noticeably shifted the strength of the party away from aged conservatism. The GOP stood for centrist policies at home and staunch anticommunism abroad. Such policies had been begun by Eisenhower and institutionalized and brought to successful fruition by Nixon. The general political debacle after 1967 did not change the perception of the

GOP as the party of RMN. The crucial intraparty fighting was over his mantle. The nomination would go to an avowed "Nixon Republican." Ford, a new Senator, was waiting in the wings, and however unworthy he seemed to some, it was his ability to promote himself as a Nixonite that gave him a second chance to run. Defeated by Kennedy in 1968, he would run against Carter in 1976.

# ★ 1
## ★ The Inspirational Presidency

This book investigates the affective aspects of politics from Herbert Hoover to Richard Nixon. Commentators on this period have focused on a president's ability to bring about beneficial change. The usual model of success is Franklin Roosevelt, conceived as an innovative pragmatist skilled at finding ways to gain his objectives. Recent historians and political scientists, themselves influenced by FDR's transformation of political life, often find their heroes in committed problem solvers and activist presidents, the architects of the contemporary welfare state. The academic experts frequently argue that this talent for getting things done justifies positive judgments of Roosevelt, Harry Truman, and John Kennedy. With some discomfort, commentators also include Lyndon Johnson in the standard pantheon.

Hoover, Nixon, and Dwight Eisenhower have been regularly classified as failures—the last also with some discomfort. I write "with some discomfort" in describing the characterizations of Johnson and Eisenhower because the concept of the "imperial presidency" has puzzled experts. Although many have praised Johnson's domestic programs, his foreign policy has been criticized, and if Eisenhower failed at home, some maintain that he did pursue admirably prudent policies abroad.

Even these valuations of Johnson and Eisenhower, and more idiosyncratic judgments, are founded on the uses of power. The experts have examined the modern presidency on the basis of what men have and have not accomplished overall, on their wisdom, or lack of wisdom, in setting and attaining acceptable goals.

It would be foolish to deny the exceptional value of the work of the many scholars who have written on this aspect of American history. There is consensus on many significant aspects of our political past, and I have freely availed myself of this consensus in writing this book. But the histories have not been without disagreement. The conventional appraisals of achievement crucial to the work of many historians, as I have already intimated, have been attacked in conventional ways. No one has constructed an objective measure of beneficial social change or figured out how to determine whether leaders were the causal agents of such supposed change. Consequently, historians have argued contradictorily about presidential accomplishment. The most striking example is of course the evaluation of Kennedy. But distinguished groups of historians have also, for example, denigrated the accomplishments of FDR and Truman or elevated those of Hoover.

The problem historians have not been able to solve is how to reach agreement on "would have" propositions. Their conflicting views of Kennedy's brief career are typical but unexceptional. We also do not know how the economy would have responded to initiatives other than those Roosevelt carried out in the 1930s, and so we don't know if what he did was good or bad. We do not know what would have happened had Truman not ordered troops across the thirty-eighth parallel and tried to unify Korea in 1950— nor what would have happened had he decided to allow South Korea to fall to the North; and so the wisdom of

Truman's decision cannot be known. Accordingly, for one historian, Hoover is the last exponent of "The Old Order"; for another he is a "Forgotten Progressive." According to one historian, FDR "achieved a more just society"; according to another, he never addressed the basic "paradox of want amid plenty" essential to capitalism. For one, Truman "will go down in history as one of the best American presidents"; for another, Truman is "a leader of limited capacity and, in the judgment of history, a dubious candidate for greatness." And so on and so on.

This book's introductory fable is not meant to hint that Kennedy was really bad, or Nixon good. Nor do I want to intimate that nothing matters—that it all comes out the same way in the end. Rather, I have wanted to engage the reader with the problem of how "would have" statements structure our understanding. Moreover, I have wanted to prepare the reader for the first purpose of the book. "Would have" statements have been central to the writing of recent presidential history. But they cannot be defended, and they are presented and contravened in standard ways. My first purpose is to examine how and why this "counterfactual" disagreement occurs.

THE second purpose of the book is to outline a way of understanding political history that gets away from conventional appraisals of achievement. This book rests on different premises from books concerned with policy. From the Depression to Watergate the resolution of substantive problems was not central to politics. What actually made leaders effective was their ability to convey to Americans that the world made sense, that the state had moral authority. Successful statesmanship provided hope and the appearance of order that legitimated effort. Wittingly or not, presidents sought to generate belief about the meaningfulness of collective life in the United States. The semblance of accomplishment may sometimes have been crucial, but not its substance. The problem of leadership was to inculcate a positive temper in the electorate, not to gain specific ends.

The health of the policy was incorporated in its leaders; if people perceived that the president was behaving appropriately, then the welfare of the social order was taken for granted. Governance revolved around the ingenuity of leaders in trying to persuade the electorate that they had matters in hand. From Hoover to Nixon, the president (and his family) incarnated the condition of American life.

In a society where the role of theology was limited, politics was religious and dramaturgical. Although history did not redeem man, politics had a sacred role. The performance of the presidency was "expressive," as opposed to "instrumental," and the political system functioned to assure the populace that the struggles of civic life had an ultimate importance. The electorate demanded that its expectations about the eternal be encouraged, and, with ceremony and liturgy, statesmen cultivated these expectations. Leaders nonetheless learned to their sorrow that creating or sustaining hope was not an easy task—nothing was so recalcitrant as the intangible.

My insistence on the subjective to the exclusion of issues that had an objective dimension does not mean that policy orientations were unimportant. The penumbra that surrounded policies and their association with leaders were crucial; but the "real" character and outcome of policies, and responsibility for them, were and remain indeterminate, as the disputes of the experts demonstrate. It would also be wrong to argue that statesmen were cynically engaged in manipulating the emotions of the public, although such manipulation may sometimes have occurred. The arrangement of feelings was not necessarily carried out insincerely, and never with facile mechanism. During this time, the stewardship of the holy was the most difficult and significant task that human beings undertook.

I would not wish to deny that from the Depression to Watergate, politicians at times set priorities, elaborated plans for carrying them out, and sometimes did carry them out. Nor would I deny that that half-century brought changes, some of which some people may think beneficial. Nor am I concerned to argue that liberalism or conservatism failed. Rather, I contend that the satisfaction of the "interests" of "the people," so far as we can understand each of these, was of the immaterial.

Political beliefs consisted in a vision of far-off goals, a moral ethos about the worth of these goals, abiding claims concerning their fittedness for our civilization, and expectations for apocalyptic success. All action depends on preconceived notions, and from 1929 to 1974 politics was a means for action that gave an aspect of complete reality to mere anticipation. It is fruitless to discuss whether political goals came true in the future. Politicians provided the hope necessary for cooperative enterprise in the present. Some politicians did this job well; others failed; but these successes and failures were unrelated in any rational way to the implementation of plans and judgments about them.

WHAT mattered in politics was not what a politician a-chieved, but how the people felt. They demanded not that goals be realized but that their hearts should react in a certain way. The mass emotion of the electorate was, moreover, not tied in any discernable way to what the experts claim it ought to have been tied to. The programmatic histories scholars have written about our recent political past are tangential to what was going on at the time.

In the following pages I stress the attitudes of the citizenry and also show in just what ways its subjective reactions at a given time may have made sense. Without judging whether the evocation of feeling ought to be a criterion of presidential success or failure, I have urged that this evocation was not haphazard, and that the public's response was sagacious. There was a logic to the forms by which politicians stirred the soul of the electorate. Historians' appraisals of accomplishment after the fact are subjective but follow consistent biases; there was also a consistency to the people's appraisals at any given time.

In emphasizing the element of common feeling, I have confronted a set of assumptions about mass democratic politics, about our belief in the will of "the people" and their moral authority. I have looked at where these assumptions lead us; but, again, I have not tried to determine if these assumptions ought to be accepted.

Historians have disagreed about the soundness of the public's views but agreed that the people detested Hoover and loved FDR; were contemptuous of Truman and revered Eisenhower; admired Kennedy and dismissed Johnson and Nixon. I have followed the consensus of historians in this matter and also found it to be warranted, but it is not always easy to determine who the public liked and disliked over the long haul. The evidence that we have at our disposal and that I have informally assembled to chart popular feeling is at best fragmentary—elections, opinion polls, and rough indicators like editorial comment, cartoons, and jokes.

The use of this evidence involves me in suggesting what we mean by "the people." Theorists of democracy want to uncover the sustained preferences of the citizenry, and voting is the formal criterion of this preference. We believe that such preference has a moral legitimacy and, indeed, even displays the general will of the republic at a given time. We believe that electoral victories express a national trend and somehow speak for the country's mood. Leaders who continue to command support are recognized as eliciting the trust of "the public."

These assumptions display a faith that we have about the validity of democratic politics. For elections hardly involve all the people, and, for example, a shift in 10 percent of those voting turns an ignominious defeat into a "mandate." Moreover, scholars have pointed out that there has been a more or less steady decline in the percentage of eligible voters casting a ballot since the late nineteenth century, when that percentage was very high. This is significant, despite the fact that the percentage of people eligible to exercise the franchise has risen dramatically in the twentieth century. Before 1920, for example, women did not vote.

Dramatically successful leadership is a matter of gaining 60 percent of the votes in an election. In baseball we understand that a supremely talented hitter may bat .400. A formidable batsman does not get on base most of the time. Similarly, a substantial minority of people are opposed to the most outstanding political figures; elections are comparative affairs in which the people's favor is given to one person in contrast to another. We presume that elections in which the victor receives over two-thirds of the votes do not reflect unusual approval but various sorts of chicanery.

Finally, it must be noted that electoral victories are not themselves unimpeachable evidence of the sustained preference of the voters. The narrow triumphs of Truman in 1948 and Kennedy in 1960 had different significances: Truman's marginal win was by far the best show of support he could muster; Kennedy's showing was by far the worst he would do. In 1964 and 1972 Johnson and Nixon had smashing victories, but neither man could hold the approbation of the electorate.

The affections of the electorate from 1929 to 1974 were not fickle, but we must also be aware that citizens expressed their views on public affairs whether or not they voted. Polls are the most salient contemporary example of this aspect of American life, but one need only go to a bar or a barber shop to see that, voting aside, people have strong feelings about matters that the experts deem political. These feelings were indicated in a variety of ways that had little to do with the franchise—polling is one standard attempt for getting at them.

THE book sets out the dynamics of the "successful" presidencies of Roosevelt, Eisenhower, and Kennedy. Roosevelt induced a faith in the American people that enabled them to live through a period beyond their ability to master rationally. Although Eisenhower expressed qualities of mind and temper different from Roosevelt's, in a different era— a vexed and troubled time—he also led people to believe that their world was whole. Kennedy's brief presidential career was punctuated with victories of prestidigitation, although his legislative record was negligible. After his assassination in 1963, many molders of opinion assumed that his leadership, had it continued, would have altered the history of the decade. The idea of "the Kennedy promise" implied not merely that JFK heroically led the nation, but also that his successors had to compare themselves to the way he, or his true heirs, would have acted. So Johnson and Nixon each ruled in the shadow of what the world would have been like had Kennedy lived.

The citizenry felt that the presidencies of Hoover, Truman, Johnson, and Nixon were deficient. Just as Roosevelt was revered because he could engender confidence, Hoover was reviled because he could not. He left the presidency in defeat, not because he was unable to end the Depression, but because he could not transmit assurance.

Truman helped to make anticommunism a touchstone of political virtue. But he could not control the issue and neither could Johnson. Historians have evaluated the accomplishments of both Truman and LBJ differently, but in neither case is accomplishment the concern. Both men began their terms as unelected presidents. The voters did not initially approve them, and each was driven from office. In enunciating his anticommunism, Truman contributed to justifying the position of men like Joseph McCarthy, who discredited Truman's anticommunism as insufficient. By making a more serious anticommunist commitment than Truman, Johnson paradoxically made the people feel ashamed of the anticommunism he displayed in Vietnam. Truman and Johnson could not convince the electorate that they deserved to lead, that the United States under their stewardship had an admirable destiny.

Nixon's incompetence was not manifested in his supposed attempt to overthrow the constitutional system, but in the perception that his rule was not what he said it was. Nixon was so maladroit at using his official prestige that his years in power ended not just in rejection but in ignominy.

The wreckages of these last three presidencies were interconnected. Truman and Johnson could not get a grip on the problem of communism that had made Nixon prominent in the late 1940s and that endured in politics for thirty years. For a brief time in the early 1970s Nixon's enemies controlled a related problem of subversion. Just as the inability to get around the problem destroyed Truman and Johnson, so it destroyed Nixon.

The sort of leadership necessary to politics from 1929 to 1974 was a rare quality. It did not prove easy to persuade a large and heterogeneous populace that had forsaken the supernatural in its daily life that its world was secure, expecially when in many cases it was not. Because of that insecurity, some readers may value the gifts of Roosevelt, Eisenhower, and Kennedy—as Kennedy said, someone who goes into politics can't be all bad. For that reason failures were to be expected, and for that reason the malaise of the American people for some time after Kennedy's death was not surprising.

THE book examines the presidencies chronologically, but it is not a comprehensive narrative. The text illustrates throughout how conflicting "would have" propositions should lead us to question histories concentrated on policy. The positive thrust of the book, however, is to trace the people's responses to their leaders. The standard focus on issues is explored from a different perspective, and the view that politics is merely verbiage or a matter of the media or of appearances is reinterpreted.

The next three chapters on Hoover and Roosevelt discuss how the patterns of mass politics (and its scholarly study) came into being. Essential in the thirties and thereafter was the way the self of the leader was manifested to a large electorate and how the electorate responded to and challenged this manifestation. The analysis stresses the way political interchange occurred. This interchange—an amalgam of the rhetoric and activity of politicians and the public's responses—was about national ideals and gave issues the meaning they had. The debate between Hoover and Roosevelt was fundamental to politics thereafter. These initial chapters examine this clash, the exemplary nature of Roosevelt's triumph in the 1936 election, and the influence of his politics on later thinking about politics.

Subsequent chapters take up different aspects of this interchange that were salient at different times. The role of policies was peculiar. They were the vehicles through which the statemen's psyches were displayed. The meaning of issues and their link to men in office were never given, but were constructed in the interchange. The chapter on Truman sees the way issues—specifically Truman's foreign policies—became the bearers of collective emotion, the medium through which emotion was expressed.

The connected chapters on Eisenhower and JFK show how the changing tastes of the people and different personalities could accommodate each other. I then look at the ironic disaster of Johnson's implementation of consensual policy to urge that a real orientation toward issues was a recipe for failure. Finally, the chapter on Watergate illustrates a negative dynamic, just as the description of the 1936 election illustrates a dynamic of success.

# ★ Hoover, Roosevelt, and the Great Depression

**F**or twenty-five years after the death of FDR in 1945, Democrats ran on his reputation. They also tried to associate Republicans with Roosevelt's first opponent, Herbert Hoover. What gave Roosevelt this clout? Why was Hoover such a failure? In answering these questions, this chapter and the next two consider the increasingly complex evaluations scholars have made of Hoover's and Roosevelt's achievements. But their divergent opinions indicate that whether one thinks Hoover or Roosevelt was good or bad depends more on one's prejudices than on the facts. What was undeniable were the feelings that the two men prompted in the electorate in the 1930s and continued to produce thereafter, and I consequently stress the logic of mass emotion that characterized politics after Hoover.

HOOVER had a spectacular career as an international mining engineer and became a wealthy man in the early part of the twentieth century. Known as "The Great Engineer" during the teens, he coordinated European relief at the end of World War I and from 1921 to 1928 was secretary

**2. Herbert Hoover and Franklin Roosevelt at Roosevelt's inauguration, March 1933.**

of commerce. The American love affair with applied science made Hoover famous. Engineering was the premier applied science, and Hoover systematically used efficiency and common sense to treat social ills. The problems of industrial capitalism, he believed, could be handled by the impartial imposition of technique.

Perceived to be "above politics" and to have fostered the prosperity of the twenties by sponsoring industrial efficiency, Hoover was regarded as the most able GOP cabinet member. In 1929 he followed Warren Harding and Calvin Coolidge as president. Six months after he took office the stock market crashed, heralding the Great Depression. For the three-and-one-half years left of his presidency, indeed for the next decade, that economic trauma was central to politics. In the steadfastness of his commitments, Hoover was equaled in this century only by Lyndon Johnson; in his lack of popularity at the end of his single term, Hoover's peers were Harry Truman and Richard Nixon.

Historians have agreed that Hoover was the first president to attack economic problems systematically at the national level, and he engaged in deficit spending in hopes of stimulating the economy. Although his efforts were contorted and failed to mitigate the Depression, they represented a departure from tradition. Hoover's initiatives were limited: he was afraid of an unbalanced budget, and, not wishing to alienate business, sought cooperation between business and government. During the campaign of 1932, Roosevelt exhibited the same fear when he condemned Hoover's deficit spending. Moreover, in the first years of his administration, FDR was also committed to cooperative action and was equally unsucessful in ending the Depression. Later, Roosevelt went beyond Hoover in promoting competition to help the economy, but these policies did not work either—recovery did not occur until World War II. The clearest way in which Roosevelt disagreed with Hoover was in the provision of direct federal relief to the unemployed. But experts disagree about whether the creation of the basis of the welfare system was good or bad. Others have pointed out that FDR undercut some "populist" legislation and that some of his legislative proposals got support from Republican foes.

We do not know that Hoover would have done worse than Roosevelt if the Republican had been reelected in 1932. Nor do we know that recovery would have occurred more promptly had FDR taken more radical measures. We do not even know if Roosevelt's policies were connected to the economic changes that did take place.

Hoover's defeat for reelection in 1932 and Roosevelt's triumphs then and later had nothing to do with these sorts of considerations—Hoover's falings and FDR's achievements—but with something more basic and elusive. Hoover had cultivated a certain civic personality throughout his adult life and it had stood him in good stead until 1929. After the Crash, however, his symbiotic relationship with the public changed. In an altered political ecology, he could not viably function. His natural reserve that had signaled dignity and restraint came to look like arrogance, indifference, paralysis, and gloom.

Hoover thought it was wrong to arouse opinion and to make appeals on the basis of emotion rather than reason. He consciously struck a pose of efficient detachment. One historian has claimed that no other public figure with the exception of Richard Nixon so deliberately adopted a particular persona. His technocratic aloofness was tied to his discomfort as a "politician"—a gladhander. "This is not a showman's job," he said. "I will not step out of character." In 1928 the electorate looked on him as a conscientious and intelligent bureaucrat who should appropriately be president in a "New Era" dominated by social scientific rationality. At the time of the Crash, the *Philadelphia Record* expressed the view of Hoover as "easily the most commanding figure in the modern science of 'engineering statesmanship'. "

Two years later the common opinion, as expressed by one citizen, was that "Engineers may be intelligent but poor Presidents." During the Depression the people demanded spiritual encouragement as well as a fighting faith, and Hoover could provide neither. He seemed distant and out of touch with his constituency during his time in office. He displayed, to the citizens, a callous lack of interest in them; being "above politics" now even took on a sinister cast. The president made the Republican federal government appear responsible for the Depression while simultaneously implying that he was unsolicitous of human woe.

The *Literary Digest* editorialized that Hoover refused to be "humanized." As one associate said, Hoover "didn't like the human element." If you put a rose in his hand, someone said, it would wilt. A reporter wrote that Hoover could "calculate wave lengths" but could not "see color." The president refused to use press conferences or the new mass medium, the radio, to get support for measures he was recommending to Congress. At the very least the president was insensitive to the trials of ordinary people. He commented that nobody was "actually starving," and reflected on how well-fed the hoboes were. When he noticed unemployed men selling apples, he explained that many people left their jobs for this more profitable one. An anonymous correspondent asked Hoover why, under his administration, "Every Thing" had "Exceptional Value . . . . Except the Human being."

Hoover had a gift for seeming cruel and heartless when magnanimity was required. In an attempt to lift the country's morale, he ate a complete seven-course dinner every evening, dressed in black tie. The greatest damage to his public esteem was done by his handling of the "Bonus Army." In the summer of 1932, twenty thousand World War I veterans camped on the outskirts of Washington and demanded immediate payment of a bonus that Congress had promised for 1945. The military marched on the Bonus Army with tanks, machine guns, and tear gas, burning the camp down and driving the old soldiers out. The assault was contrary to Hoover's orders, but he accepted responsibility and defended it. The administration also claimed that the military had not been guilty of violence and had not fired the camp, claims that movie newsreels promptly belied. Furthermore, the Bonus Army, Hoover inaccurately said, was a group of "mixed hoodlums, ex-convicts, Communists, and a minority of veterans." "Thank God," exclaimed the president, "we still have a government that knows how to deal with mobs."

Bitter jokes circulated about Hoover's personal failings. When Babe Ruth's salary rose to $80,000 despite the

Depression, a friend reminded him he now made more than the president. The Babe replied "So what. I had a better year." When Hoover asked the secretary of the treasury for a nickel to phone a friend, the secretary said, "Here are two—call them both."

The evils of the Depression became uniquely associated with the president. Newspapers used as covering by vagrants were called Hoover blankets; freight cars in which the destitute traveled were called Hoover Pullmans; a pocket turned inside out was a Hoover flag; unemployment was Hoover time; men waiting for a soup kitchen to open were a Hoover bread line; new shantytowns were called Hoovervilles. "Hoover Valley," a hobo residence in Central Park, New York City, had its name officially recognized by the city's Park Department.

"The 1932nd Psalm" went, in part, "Hoover is my Shepherd, I am in want, / He maketh me to lie down on park benches, / He leadeth me by still factories, / . . . . Surely poverty and hard times will follow me / All the days of the Republican administration. . . ."

In 1932 the president campaigned hopelessly. He regarded public speaking as an unfortunate duty to be undertaken only to educate the electorate. When he did use the radio, his voice, which many citizens now heard, was harsh and monotonous. He was the last president to write his own speeches, composing them unassisted with a pencil. They were flat and uninspiring, filled with statistics. His secretary said that Hoover, as an engineer, delivered his addresses, "as he would drive a mineshaft or construct a bridge"; they were "too correct in detail, too precise, for the casual listener or reader." The president thought he could demonstrate to the public that he was right, that his intelligence and determination to do the correct thing would win the day.

Some early commentators wrote that soon after Hoover took office his duties transformed him into "a harassed and peevish executive." His attempts to project a quiet confidence were known by his intimates to accompany fits of depression. His Secretary of State, Henry Stimson, remarked that consulting with Hoover was like bathing in ink. In 1932, especially, he behaved in a way that many found self-pitying. In time of stress his public mien was full of pique. He presented himself as an isolated and lonely leader, carrying on the fight for the nation's survival amidst what he called "hideous misrepresentation and unjustified complaint" and "little public evidence" of his good work.

The people responded negatively. Hoover had taken credit for the prosperity of the twenties, and the voters now vented their rage against him for his subsequent carelessness over their plight. He was jeered as a president had never been jeered before. In Detroit, however, crowds greeted him in sullen silence, and signs read "Down with Hoover, slayer of veterans." When he spoke there, the reports said, his face was ashen and his hands trembled. By the end of his term he was a pathetic figure, almost a recluse in the White House. One commentator noted that "The history of H's administration is Greek in its fatality."

In the campaign the Democrat was advised that he simply had to stay alive until election day, and Hoover was swamped. The Democratic margin of 17 percent in the popular vote duplicated the Republican margin of 1928. The reversal of party strenth was the greatest in presidential history.

The remarkable aspect of the 1932 election was not that Hoover was defeated, but what his defeat came to mean. He had come to personify hard times and poor leadership. The election typified many of those that would follow, in which the voters expressed their negative feelings. The president bore a national grudge, and slogans proclaimed "A Vote for Roosevelt Is a Vote Against Hoover." As in future contests, the victor gained strength because the electorate vented its outrage on the loser. One person was punished, no one else had to pay. In 1932—and for a long time thereafter—people were not voting so much for the Democrats and Roosevelt, as against the Republicans and Hoover. Certainly Roosevelt helped to perfect the art of blaming his predecessor for the world's problems. As Hoover put it, he became a "political leper." The GOP would pay for him for a long time, just as Democrats would live off the capital of FDR.

THE character of the new president contrasted with Hoover's in three critical ways. FDR lacked firm commitments and was not given to intellectual self-scrutiny. Most important, he was "the showman" that Hoover was not.

Analyses of the era are filled with comments on the ease with which the Roosevelt administration changed course or contradicted itself or moved with prevailing currents or created currents for momentarily favored policies. Hoover said Roosevelt was "a chameleon on plaid." He had perhaps fewer fixed ideas than any other man in American public life—including Richard Nixon and perhaps even Aaron Burr. Yet recollections of FDR are replete with stories of his ability to gain the loyalty of his advisers, and he frequently charmed even his enemies into submission and impotence. Although Roosevelt punished his intimates for even the slightest criticism, on many occasions he betrayed close associates. The president's personality was a political tool, his *bonhomie* a device for manipulating others in the struggles of the administration.

In his own person, Roosevelt mirrored American ambivalence about expertise. He was unreflective, and many described him as shallow, but he surrounded himself with scholars and assorted wise men, "the Brain Trust." Despite his own lack of care for the life of the mind, FDR cannily used his circle of professors and was full of guile in trading on the loyalty others felt toward him. While he may have benefitted from the advice of experts, he was not dependent on it and kept political decisions for himself; he deliberately created overlapping areas of authority to ensure his own freedom of action. Roosevelt negotiated between a vague American contempt for those who were later known as "eggheads" and a simultaneous concern to be linked with these same purveyors and custodians of knowledge.

In the parlance of a later time that came to be relevant to the 1930s, Hoover lacked "charisma." The "charisma" that he lacked was just what his opponent had. Early in his career Roosevelt learned to keep his own counsel. He created the appearance of consensus through ambiguity, avoiding confrontation and the displeasure of others by seeming acquiescence. Embued with a sense of *noblesse oblige,* FDR had an optimistic and benign view of people. He imparted an agreeable supportiveness to all around him and communicated commitments that he rarely held in earnest.

His charm, most important, extended beyond the personal and had a public, civic manifestation. But "civic charm" is a weak phrase to describe FDR's ability to expound a sense of things with which the public could identify. Oliver Wendell Holmes described Roosevelt as having a second-rate intellect but a first-rate temperament. The president's temperament, however, was far more than that. Hoover had looked on his public role with distaste; Roosevelt loved it. Anne O'Hare McCormick wrote in 1936 that "on none of his predecessors has the office left so few marks as on Mr. Roosevelt." He said himself that he gained strength "by just meeting the American people." He displayed to the electorate good sense, decency, and vigor. FDR's policies may have differed little from Hoover's, but whereas for the people Hoover enunciated them literally with sober eyes downward, Roosevelt's chin invariably tilted upward.

Words cannot express the significance of those differing images for the collective life of the polity. In a manner that still, I think, defies analysis, but that testifies to his genius, Roosevelt mastered a complex politics of hope and resentment. He conveyed a public faith yet also expatiated on public fears. He gave the people confidence but also played to their anger. He energized the citizenry. In Hoover's last address as president, he said that what counted toward "the honor of public officials" was that they sustained "the national ideals." As FDR put it, "when there is no vision, the people perish." Hoover felt that he would eventually be vindicated against what he took to be the subversive quality of Roosevelt's victory. The old president, however, did not see that it was not a matter of nourishing what were perceived as the "national ideals," but of projecting them. This was just what the new president did. No other politician could match his ability at the time, and no other would.

The modern presidency emerged under FDR. The qualities that had been connected with Hoover's rise—adherence to principle, conscientious intelligence, and a disdain for showmanship—would not be important again. Nonetheless, it would be a serious error to assume that FDR expressed just the opposite qualities, that he contributed to his office only a magnificent unscrupulousness and a higher contempt for the life of the mind. These qualities may have characterized the office after Roosevelt. But, to a large audience, the successful president had to embody the antithesis of these qualities. After FDR, opportunism and a suspicion of the intellect became, if not virtues, at least part of the regular makeup of statesmen. The essential characteristic, however, was the ability to incarnate sturdy commitment and practical wisdom. As president, Roosevelt was an oxymoronic figure.

FDR was adept at the radio talk, his "fireside chats," which brought him into the homes of millions of Americans. The people now sat "back in their favorite chairs" and heard "with their own ears the words as they come from the lips of their public leaders." After the president's death in 1945, Secretary of Labor Frances Perkins reported that people would stop her in the streets and tell her they missed the way FDR used to speak to them. "He used to talk to me about my government."

A consummate actor, as adviser Rexford Guy Tugwell called him, FDR had "a love affair" with the people. They were, the president said in the radio chats, "my friends." "When he says 'my friends,' " said Governor Tom Berry of South Dakota when he would introduce Roosevelt, "he means 'my friends.' "

H. L. Mencken christened Roosevelt "The Crooner"; another reporter said, "He's all the Barrymores rolled into one." William Allen White wrote that the president was "the old American smiler" and told FDR in 1939 that "for box office attraction you leave Clark Gable gasping for breath." Roosevelt himself said to Orson Welles that the two of them were the finest actors in America. A situation was created, Tugwell wrote, in which FDR "could do no wrong, in which his ineptness would be explained away, and in which his mistakes would be forgiven."

Hoover needed only one White House staff member to answer his mail, and from 1929 to 1933 letters to the executive from the public diminished to a trickle. FDR needed fifty people to answer this sort of correspondence. The people write their "most Honorable President," "Your honor sir and your royalty. Majesty," and "Your Excellency"; but they also referred to FDR as "my dear Friend," "my personal friend," "our beloved President," and "father of this great USA." The people told Roosevelt of the intimate details of their lives and asked for his assistance. "God bless you always"; "I will never forget you and will always pray for you and your family"; "WE WISH YOU WERE DICTATOR."

Religious motifs were striking. One New York businessman wrote in the *New Republic* "I hope God will forgive me for voting for Hoover. Roosevelt is the greatest leader since Jesus Christ." For many he became "Saint Roosevelt." Noting the pictures of the president in American homes, one observer said "The portrait holds the place of honor over the mantel; I can only compare this to the peasant's madonna."

Instead of the "1932nd Psalm" addressed to the GOP, FDR received a rendering of Joyce Kilmer:

> I THINK THAT WE SHALL NEVER SEE
> A PRESIDENT LIKE UNTO THEE
>
> A MAN WHO HUNGRY MOUTHS HATH BLESSED
> UPON THIS EARTH'S SWEET flowing BREAST
>
> A MAN WHO LOOKS TO GOD EACH DAY,
> AND LIFTS HIS TIRED ARMS TO PRAY
>
> IN WINTER AND IN SUMMER WEARS
> A SMILE, THOUGH NUMEROUS HIS CARES
>
> UPON WHOSE BOSUM SORROW'S LAIN
> WHO INTIMATELY LIVES WITH PAIN.
>
> POEMS ARE MADE BY FOOLS LIKE ME,
> BUT GOD, I THINK, MADE FRANKLIN D.

Often accusing the newspapers of bias against his administration, Roosevelt nonetheless won the hearts of the Washington press corps by attention and flattery, and through them he flayed newspaper owners and hostile papers. In an early press conference John Gunther noted that FDR struck a series of "almost theatrical" poses. In twenty minutes, Gunther wrote, Roosevelt's features expressed "amazement, mock alarm, genuine interest, worry, rhetorical playing for suspense, sympathy, decision, playfulness, dignity, and surprising charm." The president was also pleased at the response of his audience: after one burst of laughter, he "took sort of a bow with a tilt of his huge head." Speaking of Roosevelt's ability with both the press and radio, Arthur Krock concluded that the president was "the best showman."

Before Roosevelt's time political leadership had been important to a tiny economic and social group that felt it might or might not benefit from specific policies. Washington rarely intruded into the life of the ordinary citizen. After Roosevelt, the presidency became part of the daily world of the populace. The man in the office stood for the nation, and the way he was perceived to meet his duties measured the health of the country.

At the Democratic convention in 1932 Roosevelt said that the "people cannot and shall not hope in vain," and the band struck up the Democratic campaign tune for the next fifty years, "Happy Days Are Here Again." Some months later in his first inaugural FDR declared that "the only thing we have to fear is fear itself."

The Democratic song bore as much relation to reality as did Hubert Humphrey's later "Politics of Joy," for which commentators rebuked him in 1968. And what the people had to fear in 1932 was an economic system that was not working and a political and cultural elite that had little idea about how to get it working. The president nonetheless made the people believe in happy days, and he overcame their fear; they did not hope in vain.

Shortly before the election of 1932, Walter Lippmann wrote that Roosevelt was a pleasant man, who, without any qualifications for the office, wanted very much to be president. Lippmann and others later added that, at the very least, Roosevelt grew to meet the demands of the job. Many scholars have also said that an attack of polio in 1921, which left FDR crippled, deepened his previously superficial character. The presidency then gave the man a sphere to display the new depth in his soul. Other students of the period have argued, however, that Roosevelt's character was still superficial during his presidency.

The president's disease was irrelevant to his leadership. Or, rather, he was such an energetic leader that many voters were unaware that he could not walk, that he was incapacitated and dependent on others for even the minimal satisfaction of rudimentary needs. Cartoons pictured him as a boxer, as a football quarterback, as a baseball slugger—as a youthful, physically active man. At the end of a conversation, he would often say, "Well, I'm sorry, I have to run now." William Leuchtenburg, a dean of FDR scholars, reported that, as a young man throughout the whole of the Roosevelt era, he was unaware that the president was a partially paralyzed man in a wheelchair. There was an unwritten rule in his news conferences that FDR would not be pressured once he had signaled his unwillingness to

**3. "Let's Hope the Play Works," May 1933.**

Let's Hope the Play Works
    —Cowan in the Boston "Transcript."

discuss an issue. Similarly, the press tacitly collaborated with Roosevelt to guarantee that people would ignore his disability. Through the work of his aides and FDR's own determined efforts—an extraordinary cost in energy and thought—the presidency was staged to disguise his helplessness, and journalists stayed away from any mention of his impairment. FDR did not grow to meet the office. The office changed to suit him.

★ **3**

★ **Lessons of the Master**

**H**istorians have duly reviewed Roosevelt's qualities as a leader and acknowledged their importance to his success. Scholars have expended their efforts, however, in an intense examination of the origin and implementation of policy, and judgments about it. The focus has been the work of the various "new deals" in contributing to beneficial change; the programmatic stalemate of 1937–1939; and Roosevelt's conduct of World War II.

These complicated interpretations of what the president did, however, were at the periphery of popular feeling. No matter what policies were pursued, the president conspired with the aspirations of the electorate and continually evoked from it a positive response during his twelve years in office. In this chapter I concentrate on the president's most notable success with the people, his victory of 1936, to describe the communion between leader and public that he exploited so astutely.

IN March of 1933 Roosevelt began as Hoover had. The new president tried to rebuild confidence and to promote cooperation between business and government in restoring the economy. But FDR's policies meant something different to the electorate. The first six months of his administration displayed Roosevelt's activism, and stepped-up lawmaking would be a hallmark of the 1930s. The mere passage of bills—in itself suggesting change—would henceforth be positively identified almost exclusively as "reform."

The earliest measure, the Emergency Banking Act, typified the way Roosevelt functioned successfully. The banking system threatened to collapse as he took office. The president declared a "bank holiday" and immediately thereafter Congress passed the Emergency Banking Act. In his first fireside chat of mid-March 1933, FDR explained that the banks reopening the next day were sound. And they became sound: deposits returned. Now sustained by the prestige of Washington, the old system began to work because people believed it worked.

The centerpiece of the "first New Deal," as historians have called the legislation of "the one hundred days," was a program to end the Depression. The National Recovery Administration (NRA) supervised a structure of industrial self-regulation in which business and labor jointly drew up codes of employment and competition enforceable by law. General Hugh Johnson, a veteran of the War Industries Board of World War I, headed the NRA. He conceived the law as a way of promoting organized confidence. The NRA had a slogan, "We Do Our Part," and a symbol, the blue eagle. Johnson used both in the summer of 1933 in a publicity barrage of parades, speeches, and assorted spectacles to guarantee that consumers knew which merchants and manufacturers were complying with the codes. The rising tide of excitement, Johnson felt, would produce the psychological push to restore the economy.

The hoopla of the first New Deal had a vital emotional effect. Hoover had occasionally tried to lift the nation's spirits by claiming that "prosperity was just around the corner," although he had not been comfortable with such flourishes.

His attempts had been met with growing cynicism and distrust. Some historians have urged that the NRA did little to cure the Depression. Bernard Bellush writes that the NRA was "a dismal failure" and that other forces "would be needed" to push FDR toward a more enlightened approach. But Otis Graham writes that the NRA was never "given a fair trial" and that "the important structural reforms" that it "might eventually have achieved" "would have come" slowly. Whatever historians have said, Roosevelt's efforts to infuse hope somehow met with a different reception than Hoover's, as the 1934 elections revealed. The Democratic majorities again increased in Congress, the first time since 1902 that the party in power gained seats in an off-year election. Never in the history of the GOP had its percentage of House seats been so low; in the Senate the Democratic margin was the greatest either party had ever commanded. As William Allen White noted, Roosevelt "has been all but crowned by the people."

By its very nature, the economic trouble gave people a greater sense of community than they had had previously— a conventional human sentiment in the face of disaster. The era glorified "little people," "the common man," and "the man in the street." In 1932 Roosevelt shared this feeling by stressing "the forgotten man." Later he joined a platform with the aged popular poet Edwin Markham, who had long ago written "The Man With the Hoe." In the first years of the New Deal, FDR invited all people to participate in his own sense of joyous adventure and evinced courage and affection for the nation. The president's success in 1933 and 1934 was a function of his gift publicly to convey hope.

IN 1935 and 1936 Roosevelt prepared for reelection. In the "second New Deal" of 1935, historians have seen a mix of policies that proposed to end the Depression by inducing business to produce and compete and by formulating a structure of relief and welfare measures. Although considered less a policy than an expedient, relief was the administration's number one priority. The Federal Emergency Relief Administration (FERA) under the president's close associate, Harry Hopkins, distributed funds through private groups and local governments in 1933 and 1934. When FERA's initial $500 million proved inadequate, FDR took $400 million more from appropriations originally intended for more lasting public works. As the economic downturn continued, welfare became more important. The first legislative act of the second New Deal was the creation of a Works Progress Administration (WPA) established under Hopkins in April of 1935. Until its termination in 1943, the WPA performed the chief New Deal welfare functions and epitomized the various federal programs that spoke to individual and social needs.

In tracing these programs historians have inconclusively debated their justice. Who knows if welfare was desirable? Perhaps it would have been better, as Hoover argued, had many people not become dependent on the largesse of the federal government. As one historian writes, Roosevelt "smashed" and "battered" the traditional American economic system. Even FDR condemned "the dole" as an evil, "a narcotic, a subtle destroyer of the human spirit." Or perhaps it would have been better, as other critics of Roosevelt have argued, had protest not been bought off by programs that only reinforced the inequities of the existing system. The New Deals engaged in "regulating the poor," when only "basic economic reforms" "would make possible" more decent relief arrangements. On the contrary, write Roosevelt's defenders, he accomplished "more than his later critics claimed." FDR took "new departures," and "important" and "significant" positive changes occurred.

Whatever we make of the conflicts of the historians, Roosevelt's work won the immediate gratitude of many people. WPA projects especially were promoted not as relief, but as gainful work. Although the charity was thinly disguised, Hopkins built morale and gave the unemployed a semblance of dignity. "Work relief" for many people was simply a job with the government. The structure of the political economy may have been little changed, but there was a great change in the heart of the electorate.

The welfare policies were Roosevelt's version of a "warm-hearted" government that lived "in a spirit of charity." But to succeed, FDR now also drew on different mass resources than Christian love—anger and hatred. He championed the masses of forgotten people against the privileged few. The president contrasted his own approach to that of the "sins of the cold-blooded" who were "frozen in the ice of . . . indifference." Roosevelt would campaign on his attempt to help people, while rapacious Republicans—mainly businessmen—threatened American ideals.

In his message to Congress of early 1935 the president said "We have not weeded out the overprivileged, and we have not sufficiently lifted up the underprivileged." In June of 1935 he delivered a tax message that was one of the most popular in his career. Building his support with the have-nots, the president proposed what came to be called the "Wealth Tax Act" that would "soak the rich." As Roosevelt put the matter in private, it might "be necessary to throw to the wolves the forty-six men . . . reported to have incomes in excess of one million dollars a year." Congress, said FDR, had to fight the "economic autocracy," who sought "power for themselves, enslavement for the public." Americans must combat "the forces of privilege and greed." Although acknowledging that they were only a small group, the president denounced "privileged princes" and made them the center of attention. Then, comparing himself in early 1936 to Andrew Jackson, Roosevelt said of Jackson, "It seemed sometimes that all were against him—all but the people of the United States . . . [who] loved him for the enemies he had made."

Ninety-five percent of the mail Roosevelt received in response to his Jackson Day speech was favorable. "I am in complete sympathy with your fight on greed and the favored classes," said one respondent. Another wrote, "At least we have a man in the White House and not a puppet of organized wealth." The 1936 campaign, someone said in another context, pitted "pure and unadulterated greed and cruelty" on the one side, and "the crying need of a lost humanity" on the other.

Roosevelt's words came to infuriate other voters. Some adversaries of the president could not bear to mention his name. Roosevelt was only "that man," "that cripple," or "that madman in the White House." In a 1936 *Harper's* essay, "They Hate Roosevelt," Marquis Childs related how adversaries of the president obsessively talked "with a kind of painstaking delight [about] the horrible details of the intimate life of the first family." One of Roosevelt's wealthy neighbors detested FDR so much that he exiled himself to the Bahamas and returned to the United States only after the GOP won the Congressional election in 1946. In the late 1940s there was even a Chicagoan who tried to start a movement to refuse dimes bearing FDR's likeness.

The top bracket of the 1935 Tax Act applied only once in the first three years—to John D. Rockefeller. We love Roosevelt, Senator George Norris said, "for the enemies he has made." A common theme at the time was "we judge him by those who hate him." A typical statement was that FDR was admirable because "his most bitter opponents" were the rich.

Just as "the people" could not resist FDR's appeal, so those hostile to Roosevelt could not resist the appeal of the president. They took him at his word; he galvanized his enemies. Men like Hoover, identified with wealth, felt compelled to lash out against Roosevelt. Spokesman for the fortunate few found it impossible not to dispute with FDR.

When they did, they only verified Roosevelt's accusations. They confirmed FDR's devotees in the correctness of their judgment and made them even more determined to re-elect the president. Castigating his detractors as an upper-class minority, Roosevelt naturally attracted those who believed themselves in the great majority. But Republicans also attracted the citizenry to the president, their urge to defeat him ironically assuring their own defeat. By mobilizing those who did not like him and provoking them to enter the lists, the president made certain of his own triumph and their destruction. Both his supporters and his opponents brought him popularity.

A wealthy group formed the "Liberty League" to fight against a second term for Roosevelt; the organization was promptly branded "a millionaire's club." Roosevelt's aide Rex Tugwell noted that business attacks on the New Deal were "perhaps one of the best things which has happened politically." The GOP was sensible enough to try to dissuade the league from supporting the GOP presidential ticket, but the Republicans were less successful with Herbert Hoover. Knowledgeable observers noted early on that one Republican problem was "to muzzle" the former president, because his embrace meant political death. Yet Hoover had little sense at the time of what he connoted. His publicity tried vainly to build him up as "the new Hoover"—human and mellow—as he toured the country speaking against the New Deal. A newspaperman asked FDR if Hoover was on the Democratic payroll. "Strictly off the record," said Roosevelt, it was a question of "how much longer we can afford to pay." Hoover had been "so successful" for the Democrats, said FDR, that he was "raising [his] prices."

Roosevelt relished Hoover's animosity and all that it meant. When Alf Landon was later selected as the Republican standard-bearer, the one strategy FDR feared was that Landon would distance himself from all of Roosevelt's GOP foes. The president said that if he were Landon, he would run the GOP campaign by repudiating wealthy, anti-Roosevelt Republicans. Nothing would get more votes, the president told Raymond Moley, than the denunciation of businessmen and the press—then identified with business. For most of the campaign, indeed, Roosevelt ignored Landon and campaigned against Hoover and "economic royalists."

In the exchange of charge and countercharge, Roosevelt made wealth and poverty the crucial issue. More important, he was able to identify himself with masses of the less well-to-do and to identify the GOP—and certainly Hoover—with a heedless monied class. The creation of the issue and Roosevelt's identification with its positive side are all the more fascinating when one considers that the president was from an old, rich, New York family, and that his rise had been directly dependent on his social connections. Hoover was orphaned at an early age and had worked his way up from rural Iowa.

The president's adversaries could not escape the framework he had created. They tried, for example, to tie him to communist impulses in American life. This charge often proved successful between 1929 and 1974 and was perhaps more justified in FDR's case than in many others because so many radicals were at the fringes of the New Deal by the late 1930s. But Roosevelt had the ability to define the thirties in his terms. By contrast, H. L. Mencken lamented, Landon "simply lacks the power to inflame the boobs."

"The issue," Roosevelt said, "is myself." People "must be either for me or against me." "The personality of the Chief," said Vice President John Nance Garner, "is the principal issue." "Roosevelt," said Senator Norris, "is the Democratic platform." The Republican National Chairman dismissed "constructive issues." "You beat men in office, you don't elect men. . . . People vote their dislikes."

In a much noted speech at the end of the campaign in

New York's Madison Square Garden, FDR asserted that
the election was between "the millions who never had a
chance" and "organized money." The forces of money and
power, said the president, were united against him. "They
are unanimous in their hatred for me—and I welcome
their hatred." In his first administration, continued FDR,
these forces had "met their match." "I should like to have it
said—. . . ." The roaring crowd interrupted. "Wait a moment!" said Roosevelt. "I should like to have it said of my
second Administration that in it these forces met their master." FDR loved to play to the public, and in the Garden "a
raucous, almost animal-like roar burst from the crowd,
died away, and then rose again in wave after wave."

When Roosevelt toured the country in 1936, he told
Interior Secretary Harold Ickes that there was something
terrible in the people's frenzied interest in him. In Detroit,
where four years before Hoover had witnessed sullen
crowds, the cheering for FDR was almost out of control. In
New England even Roosevelt was startled by "the most
amazing tidal wave of humanity." They cried "Thank you
Mr. President!" and "God bless you!" and "You saved my
home!" and "He gave me a job!" The people were driven
to bless FDR and to receive his blessing.

The president was loved as a decent and compassion-
ate man, but he additionally expressed the polity's hatred
in a way that even later politicians like Joseph McCarthy
and Richard Nixon could not equal. Roosevelt heartened
the electorate with words of cheer, but he was also a con-
noisseur of political malice, unfailingly intuiting the vilifica-
tion people wanted to hear. People voted for FDR, but also
against Hoover, against the rich, against their bosses, if
they were employed, and against all the grievances they
had with life in the 1930s. Whereas other, unsuccessful,
presidents were blamed by the electorate for all its ills, the
people in the thirties blamed everyone but the president.
He was "the only man we ever had in the White House,"

said one person, "who is not a son of a bitch." And, said another, FDR was the only one who would understand why "my boss" was a son of a bitch.

Many of FDR's policies had elements that hardly benefitted the poor and that made them acceptable to his enemies. At times the president did what he could to thwart popular legislation. But working-class people felt better when the president lambasted the well-to-do, and the WPA gave many citizens a modicum of dignity. The electorate showed its loyalty in the election.

Roosevelt achieved the greatest possible sort of victory available in American electoral politics, a victory that also reflected sustained preference. The president received 60.8 percent of the popular vote, against 36.5 percent for Landon. Commentators had to look back to the election of James Monroe in 1820 for a comparable margin in the electoral college. States like Pennsylvania and Connecticut went Democratic for the first time since 1856. In Congress, Democrats again increased their strength. They had the largest House majority since 1856, the largest Senate majority since 1869. Paying dearly for Herbert Hoover, the GOP carried only two states, Maine and Vermont. On the bridge over Salmon Falls River where automobiles crossed from New Hampshire into Maine, some wag hung a sign: YOU ARE NOW LEAVING THE UNITED STATES.

ROOSEVELT'S presidency established the parameters of modern political behavior. The basic requirement of the statesman became mastery of the equation that linked his personality to a mass psychology, him as an individual to the feelings of the citizenry. From the Depression to Watergate each president struggled to represent positively the emotions of the whole people in his own person. This attempt was made in what I call the political interchange about subversion and countersubversion. All presidents from Hoover to Nixon participated in this blend of the administration's words and deeds and the words and deeds of the opposition, and the public's responses. The interchange hinged on what values should govern the nation and command the loyalty of the electorate, on how these values should be preserved, and on what was a threat to them. For much of the period between 1929 and 1974 the interchange was dominated by communist and anticommunist symbolism, but, for example in the early 1970s when the character of public life itself was of moment, other notions were paramount. So too during the mid-thirties when Roosevelt portrayed greedy businessmen as responsible for the erosion of the vision to which Americans were committed.

The command of the interchange that the president achieved in 1936 was unparalleled. Not only did he make his enemies out to be brutally selfish. But by shrewdly stoking

*4. "Common Ground," 1941.*

their hatred, he also got them actively to resist him. They then contributed to FDR's strength, bringing his support together in an awesome coalition. Roosevelt was able to engage his adversaries in such a way that they warranted his talk and action and consequently abetted his triumph. Roosevelt made men like Hoover accomplices to his victory. The power of the president's emotional jiu-jitsu—using an opponent's resources against him—was never duplicated.

Roosevelt did not alter business wealth and domination in the United States. He did, however, spark a debate concerning a supposed threat to the nation from the wealthy from which he gained. The conceptions of wealth and poverty that he constructed had a critical resonance in the thirties. Later presidents would emulate Roosevelt thereafter, but no one would achieve such success, and failure was a more likely result: to allow the opposition to control the interchange or to see it beyond the control of anyone. FDR's own triumph was a function of his acute sense of civic hope and civic fear, and his talent at expounding them with both craft and wisdom.

We should not conclude that issues were of no matter but we need to rethink how they did matter: they were the medium in which people reacted to the president; they were his personification, the means through which the feelings of the electorate were displayed. To understand the means we must concentrate on the interchange and the concerns that such a concentration reveals.

Let me make the main point in a different way. In elementary school, truancy is just about the worst crime a child can commit. The punishment for this behavior is suspension. Nonetheless, suspension has the same effect as truancy—nonattendance at school. That is, the substance of what happens is insignificant in comparison with the way the event gets defined. At a leading university a professor was caught in a blatant case of sexual harassment, and the university punished him by relieving him of his administrative duties, while the students boycotted his classes. As a result, the professor continued to draw his salary without having to teach or to do any administrative work, and was free to devote all of his time to research. One of his colleagues was in an objectively similar situation—he had received a great honor in the form of a fellowship that left him free to pursue his research. A central difference between the cases was the way each was labeled.

The same sort of thing was at the heart of American politics from 1929 to 1974. What made something important was the way it got defined or labeled; the "definitions" were crucial. The meaning of nonattendance at school is not given; nor is the freedom to pursue research while receiving full pay. Whether something is considered truancy or suspension, degradation or honor, depends on how people come to view it. So too in politics. The meaning of issues was not "out there." The "definitions" of politics were cultural creations that emerged in the interchange of statesmen with the public.

When Roosevelt ran for a third term in 1940, after World War II began, he was a peace candidate, just as Lyndon Johnson was in 1964. Later, in 1941, FDR used clashes in the North Atlantic between the United States and Germany to create support for his foreign policy; and in 1964 LBJ also got backing for his policies in Vietnam by using an incident in the Gulf of Tonkin between the United States and North Vietnam. Johnson's "manipulation" of what went on in the Tonkin Gulf was soon a major part of the evidence that he was an unworthy leader, yet Roosevelt paid little price for his "manipulation." This comparison between Roosevelt and Johnson—and all such comparisons—is of course imperfect. But what bears examination in each instance is not the intrinsic nature of the events, or the way one or another scholar has perceived them, but the way in which national leadership and the public struggled to embue the events with the meaning—

the cultural definitions—they had. And, as this example again shows, FDR was continually successful in turning this interchange to his advantage.


ROOSEVELT's popularity reached a fever pitch in 1936 and declined thereafter. The next year the battle over his plan to "pack" the Supreme Court provoked suspicion and showed that the president was not always in command of his sense of what the public would approve; and the 1938 Congressional elections indicated that he could not transfer his personal popularity to candidates he favored. At the same time FDR remained comfortably in control until his death in 1945. He won his unprecedented third term in 1940—"Better a Third Term" said the slogans, "Than a Third-Rater." The "workers," as one of them said, had "licked the big bosses" in 1936, and they would not later make concessions to tradition. Samuel Lubell reported that the distinction between "economic royalists" and the workingman had been sharply etched. The autoworkers in Detroit whom Lubell interviewed would vote "again and again for Roosevelt, regardless of whether it was the third, fourth, or fifth term. . . ."

The fourth term came in 1944. War has damaged the rapport other twentieth-century presidents have had with the public. Woodrow Wilson saw his leadership discounted from the election of November 1918, some eighteen months after the United States entered World War I. As we shall see, Truman and Johnson were destroyed, respectively, during the Korean and Vietnam conflicts. Yet Roosevelt won another victory after three years of American fighting in World War II. Many saw him as a praiseworthy statesman defending the verities of western culture against Japanese and German barbarism. To others he had religious significance. To still others he was a personal benefactor. For some voters FDR was a benign patriarch, adjudicating the demands of a large and unruly family. To those still taken with the conflicts of the thirties he was beleaguered but unvanquished in his battle with the titanic forces of big business. For whatever reasons, he commanded support in comparison to all alternatives. He maintained the allegiance of the electorate.

When Roosevelt had accepted renomination in 1936, he stated that the United States would "not forget . . . these years," and in closing a dramatic speech he told a huge audience of over 100,000 that "this generation of Americans" had "a rendevous with destiny." Then, to the ecstatic cheering of the crowd, FDR clasped his hands over his head like a victorious prize fighter, all the more extraordinary because the man was horribly incapacitated.

By 1940 and 1944 the president had indeed become "the champ," as popular lingo had it, and would be the champ forever after. On its return to power in early 1947, the GOP Congress made one of its first priorities the passage of the twenty-second amendment to the constitution. "The Roosevelt Amendment" prohibited the executive more than two terms in office. Republicans could not defeat FDR when he was alive; they conquered his ghost by recognizing his incomparable quality in our fundamental legal code.

# ★ 4
# ★ Roosevelt and the Structure of Politics

To the extent that political ideology was salient in the first third of the twentieth century, leadership was vaguely "progressive," believing in the joint heritage of Theodore Roosevelt and Woodrow Wilson. "Administrative progressivism," with a focus on efficiency, conciliation, and business-government cooperation was the creed not only of Republicans like Hoover but also of Democrats like Roosevelt.

The political fights of 1935–37 and the coming of World War II signaled an important change in ideology, reflected in the structure of Congress. During this period certain Democrats emerged as the principal bearers of a distinctive industrial politics identified as "liberalism."

These Democrats often came from the urban northeast and the old northwest. These regions contributed men such as Herbert Lehman, Adlai Stevenson, and Hubert Humphrey to the party; and their proposals fixed the political agenda. Liberals argued that capitalism demanded a structure of social minima—workman's compensation, minimum wages, the regulation of working conditions, benefits to the unemployed and the poor, old age pensions, medical insurance, and so on. In a complex society the state must look to the needs of the people. Liberals took up the question of planning and the right of Washington to coerce various groups to secure what liberals took to be public goods. During and after World War II, issues of foreign aid and defense joined the list. Liberals tried to gain worldwide acceptance for the policies they thought had been domestically indispensable, and they argued for large expenditures for military and economic aid.

For thirty-five years liberalism's opponents reacted to these concerns, mainly by denouncing the growth of federal expenditures and the creation of a great Washington bureaucracy. Liberalism, its opponents claimed, did not realize how inefficient government was, how it might destroy initiative and weaken the American system of individualism and freedom.

Several developments of the late thirties produced this ideological cleavage between liberals and their adversaries. The result was not just the codification of liberal views, but the crystallization of positions on a peculiar political spectrum. One major issue was the militancy of big labor and union agitation, from which FDR had unsuccessfully tried to distance himself. At its extreme, critics said, the Democratic party believed in socialism and the equal distribution of income; the party was overly beholden to workers, and it elevated class interests over the general interest. Critics also fought the New Deal because of their hostility to FDR's plan to enlarge the Supreme Court with justices sympathetic to his views. These critics believed the plan demonstrated that Roosevelt was a tyrant, debasing the American system. This view was corroborated for them in 1940 when Roosevelt ran for a third term, breaking a tradition set by the founders, Washington, Jefferson, and Madison.

The labor and constitutional controversies broke the consensus on the progressive heritage of the first Roosevelt and Wilson. A political continuum emerged containing liberals as well as their "conservative" foes. In between liberals and conservatives were various "moderates," their positions defined by their embrace or rejection of liberal notions. Initially the issues were matters like the "Roosevelt" depression of 1937 and 1938, when the weak and unsteady economy abruptly worsened. Some politicians, convinced that FDR's policies did not work, were prepared to vote for or against the New Deal on the basis of their appraisal of its effectiveness.

The comparatively mild split between American liberals and conservatives was dramatized by Stalin's Russia and Hitler's Germany. By the late thirties, conservatives pointed to liberals and implied their similarity to the communists in the Soviet Union—collectivist and dictatorial. By World War II liberals could gesture at the conservatives and intimate their similarity to the Fascists in Germany— militarist and racist. The relatively tame framework of politics in the United States was given a more extreme quality by the European left and right.

This transformation of the ideological order, however, did not mean that Congress could act programmatically, as the elections after 1936 demonstrated. In 1938, Democrats, and especially liberals, began to lose support. The result in the 1939–40 Congress and thereafter for the next four decades was a politics of stalemate. Democratic liberals set out national and international alternatives, but they were stymied in their attempts to pass much legislation, as moderates leagued with conservatives to veto liberal initiatives. At other times, moderates leagued with liberals against conservatives to thwart attempts to overturn the established domestic and international order. The New Deal's fundamentals were institutionalized into American society and foreign policy, but so too were the forces that would prevent substantial enlargement or diminution of these fundamentals. Roosevelt presided over the creation of the ideological framework in which politicians after him operated. He and his New Deal associates advanced an image of America and of its world responsibility, and proclaimed the way this image would come into being. For the next third of a century leaders of both parties marshalled the forces and rallied the troops, but they did not mount a conclusive attack. The call to colors ordinarily trumpeted the ideas of liberalism, but on occasion conservatives could impressively ask for a return to older verities and a rejection of New Deal evils. Neither side attained its goals; the behavior of each was ritualistic. What came to matter was raising the flag, frequently but not invariably in the style of FDR.

Putting aside the vexed question of how to measure the results of policies and to construe their benefits, we can say that the fragmentation of Congress from the late thirties on generally prevented the implementation of much policy at all.

HISTORIANS and political scientists have examined the New Deal and politics thereafter by adopting as analytic categories the ideological conceptions that emerged under FDR. In a 1932 speech FDR urged that the nation needed "bold, persistent experimentation." "It is common sense to take a method and try it," he said; "if it fails, admit it frankly and try another." Some commentators suggested that Roosevelt's politics thereby embraced the pragmatic "instrumentalism" of American philosophers like William James and John Dewey. According to a thinker like Dewey, it was possible to achieve a "scientific politics" by elaborating hypotheses about social life and testing them in the laboratory of our culture, with a view toward gradually generating benign situations that all might agree were desirable and productive of human benefit. As Roosevelt, uncharacteristically, put it, he had "the philosopher's satisfaction" of adjudicating matters "into the general scheme of things that are good and things that are bad for the people as a whole."

Historians have long acknowledged, however, that no such speculative intent can be found in the New Deal's policies, but there is a lingering view that FDR at least pointed politics in such a scientific direction. In analyzing this direction, historians have undoubtedly been influenced by the rationale of administrative progressivism, expounded most prominently by an engineer like Hoover. For him, politics could be subject to impartial technocratic demands. Roosevelt was not a technocrat, but for many historians his problem-solving political pragmatism had affinities with the philosophical pragmatism of Dewey.

Roosevelt described himself as a quarterback who would not call a future play until he saw how a previous play turned out. He also said that although he didn't expect to get a hit every time at bat, he wanted to achieve the highest possible batting average. The president's ideas were shared by those cartoonists who pictured him as a boxer, as well as a football and a baseball player. The sports analogies hinted that political skills led to measureable achievements in which causal connections could be spelled out.

Historians have minimally adopted a rough notion of a scientific politics in their attempts at understanding recent political history. The experts believe that they can figure out the consequences of policies and decide whether the results promote human welfare. Students of politics are committed to assessing the rational formulation and implementation of publicly beneficial policies that indeed might go beyond what is offered by practicing politicians.

Historians and political scientists believe that at some times to varying degrees the electorate votes on "the issues," but that this orientation is imperfect. Voters are often unconcerned with or ignorant of policy, and they are often swayed by emotional appeals, by a failure to grasp what is at stake, or by a lack of comprehension of the consequences of governmental decisions. Just these shortcomings give past and current political life its character of partisan prejudices and emotional commitment. As the authors of the famous *American Voter* (1960) wrote, the electorate operates through a "perceptual screen." The scholarly authorities try to overcome these shortcomings and remove the "screen."

The "nonpartisan" standard of scholars reflects a view that politics should be, and to some extent is, about reasoned accomplishment, discernable to the learned. This sort of nonpartisanship differs from partisan history in much the same way that a committed Christian interpretation of the Reformation differs from one informed by a more sectarian commitment to Roman Catholicism or Protestantism. We would surely be suspicious of an understanding of the Reformation written from the perspective of a believing Roman Catholic, but we should also be wary of an understanding that demanded that we believe in Christianity. We should similarly be wary of a view of recent American politics that demands that it ought to be, and minimally is, about the possibility of the progressive evolution of "reform" by the use of human intelligence.

WHATEVER we make of this notion of nonpartisanship, scholars have not been able to adhere to it and have in actuality been partisan in their approach. They have no systematic way of establishing the responsibility of leadership for change, or of reaching a consensus on its nature. Their evaluations regularly differ, and as I have indicated, the nub of disagreement is the different understanding they have of "would have" ideas.

The contradictory conclusions of the scholars and their peculiar inability to agree are themselves the product of the sorts of nonrational factors inherent in past and current politics. For scholars, the very notions of "issue" and "accomplishment" are tainted by the same elements that the experts contend flaw the understanding of the electorate. The experts study politics through their own "perceptual screen."

What sort of perceptual screen is it? There are many ways of organizing the writings of historians on our recent political past. Historians, however, have a favorite way when arranging readings, or writing textbooks for students. The Roosevelt presidency and what followed are discussed in ways that identify the liberal, left, or conservative orientation of the author. Scholarly writings themselves are acknowledged not to have transcended the politics they have studied.

We would, as I have said, reject a history of the Reformation that saw religious truth in the position of Roman Catholics. Yet recent history is regularly understood in terms of the political judgments that became available during the New Deal; for example, that one acceptable interpretation is that what Democrats accomplished in the 1930s was good. The partisanship of historians—the bias at work—has been political.

To defend this dimension of conventional scholarship, it is possible to argue that "politics" is an aspect of every intellectual enterprise. But then we must also confront our belief that when something is "political," it cannot be understood on its merits. We might also urge that the existence of warring "would have" judgments is not problematic by noting that there is always disagreement, that disputable values are intrinsic to discussions of all significant issues. But then we must also confront the belief that scholarship is vitiated when it reveals personal bias. These difficulties have led me to conclude in this book that our political history is in some respects flawed.

At the end of the nineteenth century, there was a revolution in the study of the sacred; religious movements began to be studied in so far as they manifested struggles for power, worldly perquisites, and psychic gratification.

Avoiding a commitment one way or another to the truth of religion, historians analyzed its functions on earth, and achieved a different perspective on the subject, distancing themselves from its categories. As Ruth Benedict pointed out long ago in *Patterns of Culture* (1934), "religion was not objectively discussed till it was no longer the cultural trait to which our civilization was most deeply committed." Scholars, however, have not yet achieved such a distance from the political categories bequeathed to us by the Roosevelt presidency. As Benedict wrote, "our dominant traits" need "special scrutiny," not because they are "basic and essential," but because they are "local and overgrown" and "compulsive" in our own culture. This book is a plea not that scholars give up their politics, but that they separate them from our history. There is no reason that political history must embody conventional political judgments.

THE most common view of the 1930s has been that proposed by liberal historians, who see the decade as an amalgam of practical, forward-looking proposals. The major interpreters have been Democrats, and the obvious liberal commitments of prominent writers such as Arthur Schlesinger, Jr., William Leuchtenburg, Frank Freidel, and James McGregor Burns scarcely need to be mentioned. These commentators believe that the New Deal flowed from a tradition begun by Thomas Jefferson and Andrew Jackson and extended by Lincoln, Theodore Roosevelt, and Wilson. Liberal historians contend that this current had a long and rich heritage; that it differed fundamentally from the reactionary Republicanism of the 1920s; and that it came to fruition under FDR. Certainly his successors—Truman, Kennedy, and Johnson—struggled to match his achievements.

The liberal argument rests on the supposed performance of Roosevelt in mitigating the Depression, restructuring business-government relations, and erecting the bases of the welfare state. What would have happened, liberals maintained, had other plausible policies been carried out would generally have been worse than what Roosevelt's policies gained for the United States. The New Deal, writes Schlesinger, was "the best answer" to America's problems; FDR, says Friedel, made his social programs workable because of "his fundamental gift" for adjudicating between "his noble objectives and the tactics of the feasible." Robert S. McElvaine adds that the reelection of Hoover in 1932 "would have been a disaster"; and that "we would be better off" if we could regain the values to which Roosevelt aspired. The argument among liberals, writes Alonzo Hamby, centers on the extent to which reforms "would have ended the depression and rebuilt American society."

Liberal historians—like Roosevelt—have been so skillful in inculcating a belief in the successes of the 1930s that more left-wing commentators have taken it upon themselves to debunk the so-called triumphs of FDR. Far more important in intellectual circles than in politics itself, the left has urged that Roosevelt was a conservative and that the reforms of the thirties were a palliative. FDR's policies differed only slightly from Herbert Hoover's and they were equally inadequate. The welfare state preserved the inequities of American life, bought off protest as cheaply as possible, and later solidified the hegemony of vested interests by giving birth, during and after World War II, to the "warfare" state. The president, these commentators assert, never took advantage of opportunities for fundamental structural reorganization. More radical programs would have led to greater benefits for the populace. Roosevelt ought to be regarded as a dubious savior of capitalism, says the left; he brought no major changes to the United States, a country still in need of a social revolution.

This leftist examination still focuses on the issues liberals and liberal historians have made central to the New

Deal. Both liberals and leftists assume that at issue is what would have happened had events been other than they were; they believe that achievement can be measured in such contrary-to-fact propositions. But the massing of evidence and marshalling of arguments do not resolve disputes. The "economic organization" put in place under Roosevelt, writes Gabriel Kolko, ignored the tremendous industrial development that "would be stimulated" by alternatives to capitalism. William Appleman Williams urges that the New Deal avoided programs that "might have transformed" America into an exciting and humane society. G. William Dumhoff writes that the New Deal resulted in "a restabilization of the system," in which the gap between "what could be and what is" remained "very, very large." Liberal historian McIlvaine replies to this notion: it is wrong to suppose "that things would have been better off had the reforms of the Roosevelt administration never occurred." And James T. Patterson argues that (in the area of federal-state relations) the striking matter is not the failure of FDR, but the limits within which he worked. The restricted alternatives meant that "it is doubtful" if other programs "would have succeeded."

Ultimately, the disagreement concerns attitudes toward Roosevelt. One side likes what he did; the other does not. For liberals what he did was just right; for the left it was not enough. That is, liberal and left historians reflect the politics of the New Deal; the way they feel about Roosevelt is at the heart of the debate.

The critique brought by conservatives is much more important in political circles themselves than it is in academic scholarship. I mean by that critique the appraisals made by men of affairs like Herbert Hoover and later by conservative intellectuals. For Hoover and those who reasoned as he did, Roosevelt regimented America. FDR, they argued, may have been something of a fascist or communist, though perhaps of a friendly sort. The New Deal was a form of totalitarianism. Under Roosevelt, the European ideas of the era migrated to America. A cult of personality subverted the ancient constitutional order. Conservative commentators complained that welfare legislation enfeebled a tradition of individualism and responsibility that Hoover would have fostered. The New Deal made people dependent on the state and destroyed individual integrity and initiative. There was, says Edgar Eugene Robinson, "a fundamental shift in the bases of American politics." The republic had been founded with a sense of the limitations of human ability, but with at least the hope for stable, moderate government. The utopianism of the New Dealers assaulted the delicate structure of a successful polity, and, says Robinson, "weakened the whole fabric of Constitutional law." Instead of removing inequities, Roosevelt's "socialistic objectives" foisted on the populace a large bureaucracy and left the country worse off then it otherwise would have been. Later, Robinson concludes, this overgrown state drifted into a war whose outcome "imperiled national security" and left the nation "exposed" to a communist threat greater than that of the defeated Nazis.

Conservatives share the belief of liberals and leftists that the president was responsible for essential aspects of American life in the Depression. Conservatives find this life and the president wanting. What FDR is supposed to have caused is at the core of each of these positions, but the language in which each talks about accomplishment betrays a subjective commitment that the others can dismiss. For liberals, FDR calibrated means and ends exactly. For the left, he dragged his heels. For the right, he did too much.

These arguments all fall within the categories that have come to define the practice of politics, and they all depend on uncorroborated evaluations. Whom is one to believe? Why should one judgment be considered more acceptable than any other? Why should the feelings of one authority about what "would have" happened be deemed more warranted than the feelings of another?

Historians rarely debate what happened; they debate the way they feel about what occurred, whether what would have occurred conforms to their ethical precepts. Their histories help to mobilize liberals, radicals, or conservatives for the battles of contemporary politics. The essence of politics from 1929 to 1974 was the attempt by politicians to juggle the people's subjective responses. The essence of recent political history amounts to the same thing—the attempt by historians to persuade their audience to share their prejudices.

In characterizing the 1930s I have concentrated on FDR's persistent triumphs, no matter what policies the New Deal tried to carry out. My concern has been the conjunction between Roosevelt's talk and actions and the people's feelings about him—the way the president intrigued with the electorate. The following chapters also explore the interchange between leaders and public that produced the social outpouring of positive or negative emotion. What made Roosevelt a hero and gave the New Deal such historical prominence was something both more and less than the goals historians contend FDR did or did not attain.

In his first inaugural, Roosevelt asserted that the people were asking for action, and action was what they got. The programs and policies of the era led to increased government activity, and New Deal rhetoric suggested that the malevolent forces in America could be curbed. Some disaffiliated groups were vitalized through direct or indirect federal support. They came to feel that they were part of the system, even though their financial and social condition may not have been appreciably aided, nor consumer purchasing power raised, nor economic expansion promoted.

The only verifiable success of the New Deal was emotional. FDR appealed to the demand for action and the antibusiness sentiment of the 1930s. It was necessary to plan and rationalize and to assemble the energies of the public even if such assembling led to nothing. It was psychologically important for people to believe that the state was working for them and against wealthy malefactors, even if the performance achieved nothing beyond itself.

Scholars on the left have complained that FDR was a master of illusion, fooling the people into thinking "reform" was occurring, even though it was not. This complaint assumes that command of the moral order—that things makes sense for good or ill—is minor or sinister. It could rather be seen as an accomplishment of merit, a victory for the human soul; it is a mean achievement only if one believes that history is redemptive or subject to rational organization. Conservatives lament the collectivist bent of the New Deal and also believe the public was duped; but they neglect to consider that the people found in Roosevelt a faith to live by. FDR's august pose so captured liberal writers that his stance of pragmatic achievement became a staple of political thought through the end of the twentieth century. Under Roosevelt the definitions essential to our politics were formulated; and, irrespective of individuals' knowledge of or interest in politics, our consciousness of who we were as a nation, of what our mission in the world was, depended on those definitions.

During a period in which traditional religion lost its hold on the nation's elite, Roosevelt offered a secular alternative. Not just Democratic liberalism, but national and international politics, became the realm in which the possibilities of ultimate commitment resided. Roosevelt became the greatest exemplar of a quasitheatrical alternative to traditional supernaturalism, convincing the electorate that his reign was justified, that under his aegis social life was meaningful. The electorate revered FDR for reasons of this sort.

To make this argument in a somewhat different way, we may say that with FDR the presidency became monarchical. Before Roosevelt, the president was not, with rare exceptions, the focus of the social order. After Roosevelt, the federal government expanded into all areas of life. The presidency became the most important institution in the culture. The moral economy of the polity became associated with the state of the incumbent. After Roosevelt, the condition of the "first family" was a national matter. Grace Coolidge (wife of Calvin Coolidge) and Lou Henry Hoover were insignificant. Eleanor Roosevelt and her children were public figures, and so too were Bess and Margaret Truman, Mamie Eisenhower, and the Kennedy clan.

The rise in prominence of the first family underscored the distinction between the public and private in politics. Roosevelt had a long-time mistress, and his wife had more intimate relations with other women than with her husband. Yet during their presidency, "Eleanor and Franklin," for both friend and foe, were collaborators in the New Deal. What counted was what they stood for, not the private quality of their marriage.

There was a similar disjunction between the public and private natures of the least successful and one of the most successful presidents among those we shall subsequently examine. Harry and Bess Truman had a conventionally harmonious marriage. Yet Truman, rarely accepted as a leader by the public, had his personal life scorned and ridiculed, his concern for his daughter, for example, made the subject of national jokes. On the other hand, John Kennedy was an adulterer, although I do not use the word invidiously, and he could not control his desires even during his time in office when it might be thought prudent to do so. What mattered was not his personal morality, but what people were determined to believe above a civic authority who was able to gain their loyalty.

At times—preeminently under FDR—leadership suc-

*5. Harry and Bess Truman with Jackie and Jack Kennedy at Kennedy's inauguration, January 1961.*

ceeded because it encouraged a belief that policies effected beneficial change. But, for example under Truman and Eisenhower, the people were much less interested in the achievement of goals; what they demanded was a sense of stability that Truman could not give and that Eisenhower could. Overall, the measure of admirable leadership was not what the president appeared to do, but how well he conveyed to the electorate that the affairs of the state were in capable hands, hands that could meaningfully order existence. From the time of Hoover to the time of Nixon, politics uniquely blended elements that are best, but inadequately, described as religious and theatrical.

★ **5**
★ **A Problem of Authority**

**F**DR was a smashing success with the people; Harry Truman was not. This chapter again explores how the president responded to the electorate and it responded to him, but with Truman, the analysis is about shortcomings. In elaborating on this motif I look particularly at Truman's diplomacy, not to evaluate it as good or bad, but to show how Truman's formulation of foreign policy involved a negative dialectic between his administration and the populace. Truman had unfortunate associations to the people, and these associations became linked to his policies. The aim of this analaysis is to consider the consistency of the public's response and to argue that issues were not the cause of the response but the vehicle in which the response was expressed.

A bookish and shy high-school graduate, Truman was raised in rural Missouri, spending his early years as a farmer. When he went into local politics in the twenties, he overcame his reticence and developed a gregarious personality. Part of the machine of Thomas Pendergast, Truman nevertheless gained a general regard as an honest and competent bureaucrat. But long before he became Roosevelt's vice president in 1945—when he was a senator in the 1930s—this regard was limited. He was considered a man of modest abilities. Truman himself was always diffident about his talents and displayed his insecurity, especially as he rose higher in the government and could compare himself to men of greater intelligence, education, and sophistication.

President on FDR's death, Truman received the sympathetic and united approbation of the people. But soon his fortunes went downhill. He was almost never looked on as a figure of stature. The president was only infrequently able to muster a fragile popularity. More often the voters were contemptuous and distrustful. On hearing Truman's first speech to Congress, one young man who had grown up in the Depression thought, "After FDR we have *this*?" Ordinary Americans regularly complained that Truman was not "big enough" for the office. He was "a little man" in the "biggest job in the world." Truman's wife said that it was like watching her husband "driving a supercharged car at suicidal speed around the Indianapolis speedway for eighteen hours a day." Truman had a middle initial, S, but no middle name, and one frustrated voter exclaimed, "They say the S doesn't stand for nothing; the whole goddamn name doesn't stand for nothing." By 1946 it was common to hear people joking "Who the hell *is* Harry Truman?" One popular slogan proclaimed "To Err is Truman." As the congressional elections of 1946 approached, another joke had it that, "If Truman were alive today, the country wouldn't be in this mess."

In the campaign the Democrats played old FDR speeches on the radio, dramatizing their uncertainty and desperation. The Republican slogan was "Had Enough?" The voters answered "yes," rebuking their unelected president. After November Republicans commanded the legislature for the first time since 1928. Their gains were the most substantial since 1920. In the Senate, GOP strength was the greatest it had been for thirty years. In the House, it was the best outcome in a midterm elections for the GOP since 1894. Many people, including some Democrats, called upon Truman to resign, and many liberals thought seriously about founding a new party.

Coming to power in the eightieth Congress, the Republican "class of 1946" consisted of some astute adversaries of the Democrats. Truman seemed no match for them, and the prospects of another, larger, victory in 1948 whetted their appetites.

No one could work up enthusiasm for the Democratic incumbent. In 1947 and 1948 Truman resisted efforts to prevent him from seeking election in his own right, while some liberals tried to secure war hero Dwight Eisenhower to head the ticket. When the general said no, however, the "dump Truman" movement collapsed. Democrats despairingly gave the nomination to someone who seemed a loser.

In a series of gifted maneuvers, Truman narrowly won election on his own, and his strategy bears recounting. The president had mastered few skills that would appeal to a mass electorate, and in particular, he was never successful as a public speaker. His voice was thin and nasal; it lacked resonance, and his enunciation was blurred. He was bad at delivering prepared speeches. In 1948 his aides worked with him and had him practice making spontaneous remarks—brief and off-the-cuff. He was trained to give natural, unrehearsed, homespun talks filled with local lore. Moreover, Truman did everything he could to run a campaign like FDR's in 1936. The new president ran against Herbert Hoover and "gluttons of privilege." The Republicans would "turn the clock back" and "do a hatchet job on the New Deal." His opponents had "a calculating machine where the heart ought to be." Performing across the country by rail on a long "whistle stop" tour, Truman condemned "the do-nothing, good-for-nothing, eightieth Congress"; and called the GOP the party of "privilege, pride, and plunder," of "Wall Street and Big Business," and of "the Hoover Depression."

In November Truman squeaked out a famous victory. At the same time some historians have argued that the Roosevelt coalition was so fresh and strong that only a major disaster could have turned the voters from the Democrats in a presidential campaign. The lowest voter turnout from 1924 to the present hinted that neither candidate could arouse much interest. Truman's popular support was better than at other times, but it was barely evident, as he consistently ran behind other Democrats across the country.

What is more important is that Truman's tiny mandate was the absolute best he could do. He never shifted the burden of defensiveness that the Republicans had attached to the Democrats in 1946. In the four years of his own presidency from 1949 to 1953, the Democrats were even more dispirited and disorganized than they had been earlier. Truman's standing with the voters went into an almost steady decline after the election and was a constant source of worry to his staff. Robert Ferrell, the most prominent historian-defender of Truman, has lamented that at the time Americans "underestimated" the man; there was a "contemporary misjudgment" of Truman. Near the end of his term, congressmen regularly spoke of impeaching him. The Gallup polls, which always made him look bad, at one point gave the president an approval rating lower even than Nixon's during the Watergate scandals.

In 1945 and 1946 the Russians consolidated a postwar sphere of influence in Eastern Europe, and excluded the United States. The administration perceived American interests there as modest but nonetheless real. Western Europe was much more significant, and the devastation of World War II posed unanticipated problems. The economic rehabilitation of Great Britain and France, as well as of the western parts of Germany, seemed excruciatingly slow. United States aid, although large by the standards of the time, appeared to be insufficient. Instead of a democratic and newly prosperous Europe, a totalitarian state controlled the east, and the west was in economic disarray, perhaps subject to left-wing internal subversion if not external communist threat. Washington's responses to these circumstances and the actions of the Soviets were the first rounds in the Cold War.

The administration reasoned that massive economic reconstruction would put Western Europe on its feet. This reconstruction was necessary regardless of the nature of the Soviet Union. Although fearful of long-term revolutionary impulses, diplomats believed that the USSR was not a military threat. Financial reconstruction of America's oldest and strongest allies—those least threatened by communism—became the focus of policy. By 1949 and 1950 the Americans did come to believe in the danger of Russian arms to Western Europe and then brought to fruition a bloc that, they believed, would stymie the Russians militarily as well as politically and economically.

The practical architect of these coherent policies was Dean Acheson, by the mid-1940s a strategic State Department official and Truman's secretary of state from 1949 to 1953. Some historians have argued that Acheson carefully played to Truman's feelings of inadequacy. In return the president, hesitant and unsure, gave Acheson control over policy, and many historians have commended his stewardship as able and intelligent. Nonetheless, many highly placed molders of opinion at the time found Acheson arrogant and insensitive and without political skill in dealing with legislators, whom he called "animals" and "primitives."

In any event, the administration had to work with difficult Congresses. Initially dominated by budget-conscious members of the GOP, the legislature did not look like it would support "give-away" programs to Europe. The administration conceived its problem to be largely one of public information: how to enlighten the citizenry about the virtues of anticommunist "internationalism" in Europe and to persuade the House and Senate to support it. But Truman was no rhetorician and Acheson was contemptuous of Congressional prerogatives. These limitations, as well as the nature of Congress itself, led the administration consistently to offer *what it believed was* a skewed account of the rationale for its programs.

At the end of 1946 and in 1947 Truman requested monetary assistance for Greece and Turkey in what became the first step in building a political and economic Western bloc. Complex circumstances surrounded the giving of aid to both countries, but the administration sold the idea to Congress by emphasizing the need to fight a vague but global threat of communism. Ranking Senate Republican Arthur Vandenberg vigorously supported the administration, and he summarized the appropriate strategy as "scaring hell" out of the American people. In a speech enunciating "the Truman Doctrine," the president made Greece and Turkey the starting points of a project ostensibly to aid "free peoples" everywhere.

Historians have debated the extent to which the administration feared a communist threat to Greece and Turkey and even to Western Europe. At least the issue in 1946 and 1947 was not the Soviet military. Rather, as policy makers said at timely intervals, impulses to social revolution in Western Europe would be nurtured by economic instability; and so financial reconstruction was the priority. Faced by obstreperous lawmakers, however, Truman and Acheson, in their minds, exaggerated the communist menace. They followed Vandenberg's notions, and downplayed the mundane politico-economic rationale that could be condemned as charity.

Policymakers worred about the need for a crude public information policy but believed there was no alternative. While his was not the only view, Acheson's was critical and gives the flavor of the approach. The ideal for the executive, he said, was a bipartisan foreign policy; and to obtain it the administration should argue that "politics stops at the seaboard" and that any dissenter was "a son of a bitch and a crook and not a true patriot." "If people will swallow that," Acheson added, "then you're off to the races." For the Democrats, a rough anticommunism was the means to ensure bipartisan support. Everyone had to be against communism and therefore in favor of Truman's policies. Nonetheless, in stressing high-flown anticommunist ideals and not the perceived needs of the entire Western political economy, policymakers were helping to build an environment in which the president would find discussion on his terms difficult if not impossible. In obtaining money for Greece and Turkey, as one scholar has written, Truman entered "a hall of mirrors."

In June of 1947, hard on the heels of the Truman Doctrine, Secretary of State George Marshall expounded an idea for comprehensive assistance to Europe. The administration attempted to argue for the Marshall Plan through an analysis of international economics. Finally, however, aided by the installation of a Stalinist regime in Czechoslovakia, the administration received the money to fight communism. Congress passed the Marshall Plan to relieve the fear politicians felt when they were prodded into reckoning with the Soviets as a world force. Truman may have had to use this prod, and in any case he could not resist using it.

JUST as Truman used anticommunism abroad, he used it at home. The administration did not invent the issue, either externally or internally, but domestically Truman reacted to Republicans urging that the New Deal was a leftist movement, "soft on communism," harboring treasonous "fellow travelers."

As New Dealers went on the defensive in 1946, Republicans popularized an anti-Democratic version of the recent past. To promote a third term for himself and to avoid Democratic defeat, the GOP claimed, FDR had taken the nation into World War II, further weakening the institutions that he had subverted in the 1930s. The totalitarian dimension of Democratic internationalism, said Republicans, was proved by FDR's agreements with Stalin. Best exemplified by the "sellout" of the 1945 Yalta Conference, these agreements ceded Eastern Europe to the Russians. Now, in 1947 and 1948, said the GOP, Democratic mismanagement—or was it more?—compelled the United States to respond to Soviet belligerence further west.

Instead of refuting this GOP story, Democrats indirectly confirmed some of its aspects by elaborating as they did the rationale not only for foreign policy but for domestic policy as well. Part of the 1948 election strategy for Truman was to isolate the left at home and to distinguish it from liberal Democracy; he would offer an alternative to Republican reaction and left-wing evil. Truman's stand between the GOP and domestic communism gave symbolic parity to a minor actor on the political stage. The president contributed to making the "Progressivism" of third party candidate Henry Wallace as important as Republicanism.

The election results indicated that Truman was ahead of the GOP in what had become a barrage of accusation and counteraccusation; but soon thereafter the president began to lose his edge. After the war in the Far East had ended in August of 1945, the United States continued to give Asia, including its erstwhile ally China, a secondary role in foreign policy. Many American diplomats thought that Chiang Kai-shek's Nationalists would lose their civil war to the Chinese Communists without an enormous commitment by the United States. Truman and Acheson were aware of this belief and ultimately did not dispute it. But the rift with the USSR gave them little choice but to uphold the Nationalists. Within the constraints set by this policy, they did try to minimize moral and monetary promises to the Nationalists and to arrange a compromise peace. Focused on Western Europe, they believed that China was not at centerstage. If China's defense required much money or, worse, a land war in Asia, the game was not worth the candle. The Americans also thought that Chiang might hang on indefinitely. Temporizing might avoid the need for difficult decisions.

This reasoning was not of a piece with the justification that warranted policy in Western Europe. If allies were granted funds to fight communism, who was more deserving than the beleaguered Nationalists? The administration awkwardly defended the rationing of rewards to China and half-heartedly anted up to Chiang Kai-shek for what it thought was a losing cause. By 1948 and 1949, the Nationalist position in China had seriously deteriorated, and by the end of 1949 Chiang fled the mainland to his island fortress, Taiwan. Assiduous in generating GOP assistance, he convinced many Republicans that the Western European thrust of the Democrats was wrong. The fight with the Russians, elements of the GOP argued, should occur in Asia, where the encroachments of the USSR were manifest and most serious.

In the milieu to which Democrats had contributed, the "loss of China" in 1949–50 thus came as a cruel blow. The Democrats now felt it especially important to demonstrate their virility. Liberalism had to compensate for the fall of Chiang and to prove that it did not appease communism. Enraged by Truman's 1948 victory and dismayed by the lack of concern for China, the GOP began its famous attacks on the Department of State.

Helped by the work of young congressman Richard Nixon, the controversial conviction of Alger Hiss, centering around charges of spying, occurred in January 1950.

The outcome of this celebrated trial devastated many liberal Democrats associated with Hiss. Shortly thereafter, Senator Joseph McCarthy asserted that at least scores of communists were holding State Department jobs at that very moment. Treason was not confined, as in the Hiss case, to the 1930s and to people with tenuous relations to those currently exercising power. "How can we account for our present situation," asked McCarthy, "unless we believe that men high in the government are concerting to deliver us to disaster?" The GOP felt strong enough to accuse Democratic incumbents. "The greatest Kremlin asset in all our history," declared Senator Robert Taft, "has been the pro-Communist group in the State Department who promoted at every opportunity the Communist cause in China."

Truman believed that the precept and example of his anticommunism was good policy and good politics. He needed Republicans to implement Democratic foreign policy and also felt a duty to keep the issue of communism in responsible Democratic hands and out of those of partisan, extremist Republicans. In using the issue, however, Truman aided its legitimation and helped to make it the measure of international policy.

Historians have debated whether this anticommunism was good or bad for the country, and the extent to which Truman bears responsibility for creating the issue. His critics argue that he was an accomplice, even if unwitting, of McCarthy. Truman, they say, made matters worse than they otherwise would have been. The president's defenders claim that he did what he could to cap an irrational movement, and that things would have been worse without his comparative restraint. A significant factual matter is usually overlooked in this inconclusive politicized argument: Truman could not control anticommunism. His enemies used it to destroy his authority with the electorate and to drive the Democrats from the White House.

THE administration initially tried to defuse McCarthy's charges through the appointment of Millard Tydings, a conservative Democrat, as head of a Senate committee examining McCarthy's evidence. Tydings was assisted by a diplomatic victory for the White House. In June of 1950 the communist North Koreans launched an attack on the American client state of South Korea. Truman's forceful and immediate response—a United Nations "police action" led by the United States—promised to repel the invaders and restore the *status quo ante bellum* at the thirty-eighth parallel, the dividing line between North and South Korea. The administration thus showed its determination to halt Asian communism. Tydings relied on Truman's strong position to imply that McCarthy was grossly misrepresenting Democratic attitudes toward communism. Truman's popularity went up for the first time since the beginning of his second term.

As Acheson suggested, the stakes in Korea were about prestige, "the shadow cast by power." But acting now to protect something intangible, the administration lacked the subtlety to succeed with the public.

The American leader in the Far East was Douglas MacArthur. Acknowledged to be brilliant, but also thought of as erratic and overweening, he believed that the future lay in Asia, where he had a mission to free its peoples from communism. Friendly with congressional Republicans of the right, MacArthur was a dangerous man for Democrats to rely on.

After initial victories by North Korea, forces under MacArthur fought their way up the peninsula. After a tactical coup by which he recaptured the South Korean capital of Seoul, MacArthur had the North Koreans on the run. The battlefield victories in the early fall of 1950 justified Truman's response to the crisis and boosted the administration's—as well as MacArthur's—reputations. Additionally, the Democrats thought that the crisis could be managed for domestic political gain and could bolster foreign policy in Western Europe.

In April 1950 the administration completed a reappraisal of defense policy. A National Security Council Report (NSC–68) outlined a Soviet military menace in Europe. Having come around to the Republican orators' view of the danger of Russian communism, however, the Democrats wanted to meet the danger. They called for a quadrupled defense budget. How were they to get the appropriations? The GOP might have lambasted the administration for softness on communism, but it did not advocate spending huge sums on defense, and it noted the unwillingness of Europeans to spend for their own defense. The Democrats were more serious about anticommunism, but they faced the same old problem: how to extract money from the Republicans in Congress. Acheson again noted the need to overstate what he thought the Russian challenge to be. The idea was "to bludgeon" legislators. Policymakers, said the secretary, were not writing Ph.D. dissertations, and matters had to be made "clearer than truth."

Administration Democrats believed that the attack on South Korea was a Soviet feint, perhaps a prelude to a more serious encroachment in the West. Nonetheless, a strong response in Asia would not only demonstrate liberal toughness but also provide a climate in which the defense budget would be expanded in the aid of the European policies. "We were sweating," over NSC–68, said an Acheson aide, and, then, "thank God Korea came along."

Money for defense that Congress allocated in the summer of 1950 was funnelled to Western Europe. Moreover, the wartime urgency promised that the requirements of NSC–68 might be fulfilled. Liberal historians and those of the left and right have variously interpreted these Democratic ideas, and there is no consensus. The American response was prudent and checked what would have been serious communist encroachments; the United States

"made good a stand against aggression and . . . appeasement." The response "in its cynicism, destructiveness, and
illusion" was "an introduction" to the "most sustained crisis
of the modern American experience—Vietnam." The notion of "limited war" was weak, and we would have done
better to take a strong position against China. Even if everything had gone well fighting such a war, it is questionable if
the United States "would . . . be able to avoid" frustration.
Who is to say?

What is factually critical was that Truman and Acheson tied their fortunes to MacArthur. Elated by battlefield
conquests, the prospects for more, and the political profit
to be made from them, the administration acceded to and
even promoted MacArthur's request to take the fight into
North Korea. In the latter part of 1950, Truman was additionally aware that the GOP would accuse him of appeasement if his position were moderate, and the international
tension justified what he wanted in Europe. Unification of
Korea by Western power was beguiling. The aim of restoring the *status quo ante bellum* was forgotten.

As United Nations troops rushed north in September
of 1950, American audacity seemed to have been rewarded.
The administration demurred at MacArthur's ill-concealed
desire to cross the North Korean–Chinese border at the
Yalu River and to carry the war to China. Truman also bore
with MacArthur's playing politics with the GOP. He sanctioned, however, the goal of freeing all of Korea, despite
warnings by the Chinese that they would not tolerate a hostile presence on their border. In November, their warnings
ignored, the Chinese counterattacked.

In Korea hard choices faced the Democrats: to conduct
a cautious rebuff of the north and confront Republican ire
about Democratic weakness; or to join with MacArthur and
to outflank their domestic foes. Each alternative was risky.
Nevertheless, by the second half of 1950, in the context of
domestic politics, the administration responded by shield-

ing its own preferences in Western Europe with the crisis in Asia.

The war changed when the Chinese entered it. Through the late fall and early winter of 1950, the United States suffered a series of humiliating defeats as it was again pushed below the thirty-eighth parallel. Truman had gambled that he could extract an anticommunist coup from a crisis of real but modest proportions. By early 1951 he looked forward, abroad, to a long and serious encounter with China and, at home, to renewed GOP cries that the communists were on the move.

In April of 1951, Truman fired MacArthur. The domestic storm that was raised testified to Truman's diminished status. MacArthur's replacement, Matthew Ridgeway, began to move American forces back to around the thirty-eighth parallel. Truman and Acheson agreed that there the noncommunist troops should stop. The damage, however, was done.

At the end of 1950 many called for Acheson's resignation and there was talk of the impeachment of the president, talk that resumed after the dismissal of MacArthur. Republican Senator William Jenner said that "this country today is in the hands of a secret inner coterie . . . directed by agents of the Soviet Union. Our only choice is to impeach President Truman and find out who is the secret inner government." "The son of a bitch ought to be impeached," said McCarthy.

Playing on the public's feelings of resentment and frustration, McCarthy stoked public distrust and hatred to a level that had not been seen since Roosevelt's attack on the wealthy in the mid-1930s. McCarthy engaged in a ritual of degradation in which all of those who were "wrong" about FDR would be purged. Americans engaged in a psychodrama of mystery and revelation, involving imputations of guilt and protestations of innocence. Against this backdrop, the administration dealt with a crisis of ambivalence in the populace about Korea, between support for the troops and doubts about the war, between militant anticommunism and the fear of escalation.

The result was that in 1951 and 1952 the Truman administration was discredited, domestically and internationally. The president was unable to shape what he took to be real concerns in the United States and around the world. In late 1951 his popularity went to 23 percent, a record low. By the spring of 1952 it was still only 26 percent, and many Republicans were still calling for his impeachment.

FOREIGN policy, I believe, is the critical area in which to see how Truman lost control of the polity. For the information program he promoted in international affairs got Truman into difficulties in publicizing his real views; and this same program had consequences for Truman's ability to stay ahead of the GOP at home. By 1951 the ever-more-elaborate mix of foreign policy demands, misstatements about programmatic aims, and domestic considerations had not only mired the United States in Korea but had also seen Truman hit bottom in the estimation of the public. Nonetheless, it would be a mistake to assume that the desperate straits of the administration in the early 1950s involved only foreign policy. Truman was also hurt by assertions that he harbored crooked employees and that he was a usurper of executive power.

The various scandals that shook the administration began in the middle of 1949, but regularly punctuated national politics until almost the end of Truman's elected term. Historians have made little of this aspect of his presidency. At the time, however, the corruption—involving conflicts of interest on the part of office holders in the executive—was conventionally compared to what went on under Warren Harding in the "Teapot Dome" scandals. By late 1951 a vocabulary of catchwords emerged to describe Truman's circle and to raise public indignation—croneys, influence pedlers, five percenters (the amount of the "rake-off" the crooked employees were supposed to have gotten).

The administration was reeling from the scandals when it took over American steel mills in early 1952, to avoid, it said, a crippling strike and to maintain defense production. Truman hoped he could focus public attention on the patriotic need for the continued output of steel during a war. But when the steel companies took the government to court, Truman lost another battle. One newspaper headline read "Truman Does A Hitler," and the Democrats had to defend themselves against accusations of dictatorship. When the Supreme Court ruled against the government, Truman promptly returned the mills to their owners, but he also lost in the court of public opinion. One authority writing on the case has claimed that it was a critical precedent for the court cases of the early seventies, centering on President Nixon's role in the Watergate burglary. Another authority has argued that the steel seizure was the most important instance of the misuse of executive power before Watergate. In any event it looked at the time like Truman had recklessly overstepped constitutional boundaries.

Communism—domestic and internation—and scandal, and a legal crisis all contributed to the president's low standing in 1951 and 1952. Preparing for the election of 1952, the GOP adopted the "$K_1C_2$" formula—Korea, communism, and corruption. The Republican nominee, Dwight Eisenhower, said the issues were "the heavy burden . . . of a party too long in power." Eisenhower was a major factor in the Democratic debacle that came in November. Yet, historians have argued, almost anyone could have defeated the Democrats, as they tried to distance themselves from Truman. Faced with almost certain defeat, the president apparently considered running a second time and then withdrew from the race. Democrats

breathed a sigh of relief. When Truman decided to help
Adlai Stevenson, who had to campaign against the slogan
"Want Another Truman?" the Democratic nominee shud-
dered. Indeed, Stevenson—as well as Eisenhower—promised to clean up "the mess in Washington." As usually
happened in elections, politics was a vehicle for expressing
rage; the people voted against the Democrats; Eisenhower
gained in stature as the people made Truman the lamb
sacrificed to their frustration. Only twice since 1928 has
the GOP captured both houses of Congress. In 1946 and
1952 voters repudiated the beginning and the end of the
Truman presidency.

HISTORIANS have differed in their judgments of the necessity, justifiability, and wisdom of the Truman administration's anticommunism. In the 1960s and 1970s leftist historians berated Truman as a vulgar cold warrior whose policies
presaged what the left saw as the evils of the Vietnam era:
had he behaved otherwise, the United States would not have
been placed on the path that led to Vietnam. Athan
Theoharis writes that Truman was responsible for "repressive and unfair" policies that "would have been bitterly re-
nounced" and "would have been rejected" in 1945; and
Richard Freeland writes that a different approach from
Truman's "would have allowed" the administration to be
more effective against extreme anticommunism. The left
believes, writes liberal historian J. Joseph Huthmacher, that
even had all of Truman's policies been successfully imple-
mented, the result "would still have fallen far short of solving the real problems that beset American society" in the
period. But left historians cannot demonstrate that Truman
was responsible for the cold war or that it was an avoidable
evil. Indeed, the leftist interpretation was immediately challenged by more liberal historians in the 1970s and 1980s.
For these scholars, Truman consolidated the blessings of

the New Deal and heroically led the nation against the Soviet menace; without Truman's firm action, Russian successes would have multiplied. And, writes Earl Latham, "the evidence" is that in the absence of Truman's anticommunism, the GOP "would have forced" even more painful measures on the nation. In any event, says Alonzo Hamby in responding to the left, it is "unrealistic to assume that the Truman administration should have anticipated the central concerns of the sixties and seventies. . . ." This evaluation, however, is as dubious as the one made by the left: there is no way of proving that American foreign or domestic policy was benign.

There is no objective reason to assert that the messianic anticommunist accent in which the administration often spoke was either good or bad. At least with the voters, all of the administration's work might have availed had Truman more adroitly managed the public trust. The president, however, could not dominate the 1940s interchange of subversion and countersubversion and could not prevent the GOP from stealing the emblems of authority from him. At no time did he take any step that seemed wildly inappropriate. Yet to stay ahead of his opponents he engaged in increasingly complex decisions that linked foreign and domestic policy to his public information campaign. As the administration resorted to more complicated strategies, its perceived incapacities became the target of civic contempt. By the end of his term, American politics was dominated by an anticommunist view beyond Democratic control. Indeed the emblems of authority eluded the control of almost everyone.

FDR never mastered the tangible issues of the 1930s, but he did master the eloquence and drama of the decade. Truman was ill-equipped to inherit the sort of regime FDR had created. The electorate was accustomed to have the president give significance to national life and was disgruntled with what Truman signified. The president had a con-

sistent understanding of what he took to be the real problems of his era, but by its end, the crucial problems were
insubstantial, and he could never bring them under his juris-
diction. Perhaps Truman could have done nothing different. Nonetheless, the failure from which he could not escape was his lack of skill in conveying a satisfying sense of
public life to the people.

WHAT was the president's problem? Unlike FDR, who loved
his job, Truman regularly expressed his discomfort with his
official duties in letters that were not sent, memoranda written only for himself, and various private communications.

A memo from November 1945 displayed many of his
frustrations about the world. To solve his problems, Truman would declare an emergency, call out the troops, ad-
journ Congress, jail dissidents, shoot labor leader John L.
Lewis (a man Truman hated), and drop the A–bomb on
Stalin. His private despair over foreign policy continued
throughout his years in office, culminating in an unsent
ultimatum to Stalin of early 1952. The Russians were to get
"the Chinamen" out of Korea; to free Estonia, Latvia, Lith-
uania, Poland, Rumania, and Hungary; and to stop foment-
ing revolution; or face "all-out war" in which every major
city and manufacturing plant in China and the Soviet
Union was to be "eliminated."

Truman's irritation was not limited to international
concerns. His private expressions of pique have become
common knowledge. Two Democratic representatives
from his hometown's congressional district were "double
barrelled shit asses"; his Senate leadership did not have
"the guts of a gnat"; doctrinaire liberals were "the lowest
form of politician"; Senator William Fulbright was "an
overeducated Oxford SOB"; Senator Estes Kefauver (another pet peeve of Truman's) was an "intellectually dishon-
est" "demogogic dumb bell": Senator Paul Douglas was "a

crackpot"; Henry Morgenthau, jr., his early secretary of the treasury, was a "blockhead" and a "nut"; former Secretary of State James Byrnes was a "political whore"; and Adlai Stevenson's 1952 campaign was run by "crackpots" and "high socialites."

The president detested having to deal with the press, with whom he had continual nasty fights. Reporters were "liars and blackmailers," "prostitutes of the public mind," and "mental whores." *Time, Newsweek,* and *U.S. News and World Report* were "slick purveyors of untruth." He made many scathing appraisals of prominent journalists. William Randolph Hearst was the "No. 1 whore monger of our time"; Westbrook Pegler "the greatest character assassin in the United States" and "a louse"; Walter Lippmann, said Truman, would do better working in a latrine than in an ivory tower. In the most famous public incident, which made Truman appear simply petty, he attacked critic Paul Hume and threatened to punch him for unfavorably reviewing his daughter Margaret's singing. Hume, said Truman later, was a "frustrated old fart."

The president characterized almost all who crossed swords with him as "cheats," "crooks," "doublecrossers," and—his favorite expression—"sons of bitches" who could "go to hell." His private writings were filled with denunciations couched in images of female promiscuity and scatology.

What did this dimension of Truman's character mean? Certainly it meant that he was ill-equipped to perform any of the priestly functions of his office. The president's problem, I think, was a limited confidence about his worthiness for the presidency. He oscillated between cocky determination and impetuous quarrelsomeness, between caution and brash assertion, as if proving something to himself. Sometimes he may have been forced to take bold action because matters had been allowed to drift irresolutely for a long period. His need to protect his self-respect made him, the President of the United States, lash out at minor adversaries, thereby diminishing the people's respect for him. These sorts of issues rarely lessened FDR, Eisenhower, and JFK in public.

Truman's character was critical to his more general inability to mold civic, and even private, perceptions. On many public occasions his anger was translated into a lack of verbal restraint. These outbursts usually resulted in unfortunate embroglios; Truman came to look like a blunderer when he later had to retreat from what he had said. The president recounted that he had adopted a similar "tough" approach in many face-to-face confrontations with adversaries, and in old age his crusty persona was legendary. But the recollections of the president's opponents and, more important, contemporary records often do not corroborate Truman's image of himself. The denunciations of his foes, when they were not around, as often as not were matched with expressions of uncertainty in their presence. After someone had left his office, one aide reported, Truman would say, in effect, "I certainly set him straight" or "I let him have it." But, the aide recalled, "the president's remarks seemed to me to have no conceivable relation to the conversation I had just heard."

The president was regularly afraid of projecting his power. When he tried, his exertion too frequently came across in private or to the people as bluster or bumptiousness. He was unable to solve the equation connecting his ideas and the public presentation of them that would have allowed him to maintain the confidence of the electorate.

The president intimated this himself. "I'm not big enough for this job," he early told a Senate friend. "You know," he would tell his staff during the early years, "I'm not an elected President." At the end of 1947, he blurted out about the crippled Roosevelt "I'm not a superman, like my predecessor." His victory in 1948 did give Truman more security and made him feel more chipper. But this was a mixed blessing: assertiveness did not make him more effective with the people—indeed, less so; even 1948 did not give him much security. Toward the end of his elected term, he said that "a great many people," "maybe a million," could perform the duties of the presidency better than he, and he regularly expressed reservations and complaints about the job. One historian has written that the persistent criticism Truman received over trivial matters made it plausible for him to consider himself "a national scapegoat."

These failings as a leader were heightened by Truman's unreserved partisanship. The president had difficulty seeing that any criticism or opposition to him could be warranted; and, like Herbert Hoover, he always felt abused and misrepresented. In this respect, he was myopic. When the scandals beset his administration in the early fifties, he coped with them poorly. The president saw attacks on his subordinates as personal attacks on him. He was unable to separate himself from inconvenient people, or to rise above personalities. The electorate saw this, and responded accordingly. Truman appeared complacent, oblivious to simple justice, and an exponent of government by croneyism. The president could not see that his administration appeared sleazy and that the aura of crookedness dishonored him with the public. He lacked the sensitivity that would have enabled him to grasp how the conduct of his associates reflected on him. He never realized how they appeared and how he was devalued.

In these ways Truman was much like Richard Nixon, a comparably unpopular leader driven from office. Nixon was a battling partisan, uncertain of his worth and hating the press. He left the presidency because of scandal and the fear of subversion.

Truman's problem was that he lacked authority. The people saw this almost immediately and were unwilling to give him the benefit of the doubt, no matter what the undertaking. He was insecure, and the electorate was insecure with him. Although historians have been unable to reach agreement about Truman's policies, the people had no difficulty agreeing on the President's failings. They were suspicious of him from the start, and basically they found their suspicions confirmed during his eight years in office. By 1951 and 1952 when Truman was attacked about communism at home and abroad, about corruption, and about executive usurpation of power, the people were suspicous of him no matter what he did. The president got into trouble regardless of the decisions he made; he found it impossible to get on the right side of an issue. He entered into—indeed, as president helped to create—the political interchange about the nature of virtue in the United States, the future of the country, and the character of American ideals. But in contrast to FDR, who had the nation playing to his tune, Truman could rarely catch the rhythm of the people. The polity expressed its frustration—even fury—at Truman's tone deafness through negative evaluations of his policies, but nothing about the man pleased voters. Public reaction to the president ran deeper than the issues.

Truman the person was the target of the people's wrath. It is useful to note that whatever historians have made of the substance of his administration's international programs, the form of these policies was congruent with Truman's character. There was the same mixture of straightforwardness (the campaign against GOP foreign policy in 1948) and lack of straightforwardness (in dealing with Congress), of assertiveness (the Truman doctrine) and timidity (yielding over aid to China).

By the second half of his elected term, these structural elements of public policy and his personal character came together. Truman unhesitatingly chose to fight in Korea, then made more of the war than his conception of its importance justified; the president moved north of the thirty-eighth parallel seemingly without regard for consequences, yet hesitated for months to deal with MacArthur. In early 1951 the actions of the administration were the means through with the electorate reacted against Truman. The style of national action reflected the problems in the president's personal manner.

There is much for liberals and liberal historians to speculate about in this analysis. Truman refused to step down in 1948. The result was that the guardianship of the symbols of the state in the early 1950s passed into hands that many liberals believed were less decent and well-meaning than his. Had Thomas Dewey and the Republicans won the election of 1948, the 1950s might have been presided over by a man whom liberals believed to have greater ability than Eisenhower. Had the Korean War occurred, it might have been more readily contained by someone like Dewey and so perhaps might Joseph McCarthy. The Democrats were shamed out of office in 1952; a Truman defeat in 1948 might have been less wounding.

The details of Truman's dilemma point to a more gen-

**6. Harry Truman, November 1948.**

eral consideration in the study of politics from 1929 to 1974. Historians have not been able to establish the caliber of the foreign policies of his administration in a way that commands assent. The diversity of opinion among knowledgeable interpreters about the efficacy and goodness of the administration's approach suggests that there is no link between the nature of policies and the responses to them. Indeed, it is a mistake to think that policies have natures that may be causally connected to the approbation of the electorate, or to that of later inquirers. The essence of policy is not given; it is fabricated in an interchange between the presentation of policy and those to whom it is presented. Historians later engage in a similar confrontation when they investigate and evaluate past policies. Their error, however, is twofold. First, instead of concentrating on seeing how things were to the public at the time, they have concentrated on figuring out how things are to them and have assumed that that is how things were. Second, historians have implied that their techniques are justified because policies have an objective aspect, no matter how great the failure of scholarly consensus. Yet the character of policies is not "there," but is truly in the mind of the beholder.

A more appropriate way to look at the issue orientation of politics is to understand that issues were the vehicle through which feelings were expressed. Mass emotions were never displayed without being attached to issues—the latter were necessary to the former. The issues nonetheless did not determine the visceral response. That response was the product of something much more elusive—a collective feeling about the man in office.

# ★ 6
# ★ Moment of Certainty: 1953–1960

Eisenhower and Kennedy differed. Their party affiliations were at odds. One was a midwestern Protestant, the other a Boston Catholic. Old and avuncular, Eisenhower was almost thirty years senior to Kennedy, who exuded sexual vitality. The general saw himself as a prudent conciliator; the civilian adopted an assertive, even aggressive, approach. Yet each man was, in his time, triumphant with the American people. Effective policymaking does not explain the triumphs. Whatever commentators make of the problem, they have noted that neither president was much interested in domestic issues. Eisenhower dealt with Democratic congresses and could not get much of a program through. Kennedy also had no luck with a program at home—one historian has written that JFK's relations with the legislature were worse than those of any president since William Howard Taft. Commentators have stated that in foreign affairs these two presidents were disparate. Even although their evaluations conflict, the experts agree that Kennedy was an activist, Ike more cautious. One should not even stress that each leader in turn dominated political conversation from 1953 to 1963, for in this period that interchange was muted. Rather both men simply appealed to their publics.

Eisenhower responded to and reinforced basic satisfaction in the electorate. Kennedy responded to and reinforced unease and a demand for reassurance. This chapter and the next examine the men and the changing circumstances that gave the decade its solidity, and consider the success of these two men in the context of what came before and what followed.

FOR some time after the end of the Eisenhower administration, liberal commentators dismissed the 1950s as a sterile period. William Shannon said that the fifties were "the age of the slob." and in "Good-Bye to the 'Fifties—and Good Riddance," Eric Goldman wrote that Eisenhower's time was "the dullest and dreariest in all our history." Left historians have been puzzled by Ike. They admire his caution in foreign policy, at least in comparison to what they see as the excesses of Kennedy and Johnson, yet they dislike his conservative policies at home. Blanche Wiesen Cook writes of the "divided legacy" of our "most undervalued" president, but Howard Zinn complains that although postwar interventions were carried out by Democrats, "conservative Republicans like Eisenhower" supported the interventions. Impressed with what they perceive as Eisenhower's genuine prudence, more conservative scholars applaud the man, as Robert Divine puts it, for the "moderation and restraint" that kept him from "abusing the power inherent in the presidency." Eisenhower was skilled in avoiding confrontation and disunity; he pursued his goals with quiet skill, an exponent, one book says, of "the hidden-hand presidency."

Although there is no clear way to choose among these alternatives, they do share two characteristics. First, these authors believe that their appraisals are based on wisdom and calculation in the use of power, despite the fact that there is apparently no unprejudiced way to measure the correct use of power. Second, these scholars are bemused by the president's unflagging popularity as a hero during his incumbency. There is something to be said on all sides of the issue of the man's achievement: what is beyond dispute is the affection that the American people felt toward him.

Walter Lippmann commented that Eisenhower was a chaste vessel "into which the public would pour all its hopes." Emmet Hughes wrote that Eisenhower's "easy air of personal authority" was a "physical fact [that] symbolized a political fact." And James Reston added that the esteem in which Eisenhower was held was "a national phenomenon, like baseball." It was not "just a remarkable political fact but a kind of national love affair." As one close associate put it during a foreign policy crisis in the late 1950s, the president was important because he gave to others "an impression of unruffled assurance and confidence."

Genial and sincere, Eisenhower was also a shrewd man who elevated himself above politics; he was the most successful president except FDR, the only one after Roosevelt to serve out two terms. His first victory in 1952 was partially a vote against Truman, but his second, again over Adlai Stevenson, was a rarity—a vote for the person himself. The death of Senator Robert Taft and the waning of McCarthy's power left Eisenhower without a rival in the GOP. At the same time the strength of the party as a whole came to a head in 1952 and declined thereafter. In 1952 the general ran 19 percent ahead of other Republican candidates. The 1956 election was the first since 1848 in which both the Senate and House were in the hands of the party that had lost the presidency. From 1952 to 1959 the GOP lost 24 percent of the total offices it held. In 1958 the number of GOP Senators was reduced from a 1951 high of 47 to 34; in the House the number went from 199 to 153; these were the largest Democratic margins since Roosevelt's 1936 victory. In governors' chairs, GOP strength went from 25 to 14. In 1957 Theodore McKeldin, governor of Maryland, said that the GOP had nothing the United States wanted except Eisenhower. But that was enough. He gave his name to the era.

The president's appeal in a period of waning Republican fortunes elsewhere testified to the electorate's lack of concern for policy. The public did not care to grant the president power to effect a program. Eisenhower himself showed only modest commitment to a programmatic course, and he had little success in promoting his own brand of "modern" Republicanism as the rallying point for budding GOP statesmen. Yet the people obviously desired Eisenhower as their leader. "The less he does," said one *New Republic* writer, "the more they love him." The 1952 electioneering slogan, "I like Ike," became "We like Ike."

Running World War II in Europe had been an exercise in conciliation for Eisenhower, running a large bureaucracy. He had been the army's number one public relations figure, a simple soldier of democracy then first known to millions of Americans as "Ike." He later brought his ideas on management to government and his style to the White House. He had no sense that Washington should provide an alternative vision to business leadership. To the extent that he thought about the issue, he believed that the state should not enunciate a collective ethic. His concept of the moral role of the executive was limited. The president, he said, "should stand, visible and uncompromising, for what is right and decent." "Decency," he added, "is one of the main pillars of a sound civilization. An immoral nation invites its own ruin." Eisenhower forsook the notion that the presidency was a pulpit, except insofar as he could comment on individual virtues. Throughout the period there was a remarkable absence of either the strident language that had preceded him or the soaring language that followed, and federal activity at least appeared more limited. The state should not encourage any civic responsibility except what was already embodied in the lives of successful citizens. For a public exhausted by the clamor of the Truman presidency, this was exactly right.

The people wanted to feel at ease. Eisenhower believed that they sought a breathing space after the long Democratic era. In announcing the Korean ceasefire in July of 1953, he resisted making the long battle even resemble a crusade. "The war is over," he said, "and I hope my son is going to come home soon." He sanctioned a turn to the exclusively private life and inculcated the notion that the store needed little minding.

Eisenhower communicated that his presidency would be nonimperial. Official duties would not interfere with hunting, bridge, and golf. He was the first TV president, and projected control through managed press conferences and televised speeches. Things were easygoing, and Ike seemed to preside over a tranquil, if not soporific, period.


FDR was elected four times because he allowed the people to believe that the nation was being governed competently. In a different era, Eisenhower was similar. A "father figure," as the popular psychology of the time had it, Ike took an approach that justified a public moral holiday because there was nothing much to worry about. At the same time, changes occurred in the 1950s. The Korean War ended on terms that had been politically impossible for Truman to accept. Eisenhower oversaw the downfall of McCarthy and healed the wounds in the GOP. He waged the Cold War, and he witnessed the rise of an incipient civil rights movement. Ike did not urge an end to the New Deal, and it became palatable to everyone. The president did not plan these changes, but he did encourage the view that events were self-regulating. During this time he came across to millions as a personal moral leader.

Roosevelt's impact on modern America was so great that many pundits have supposed that the sole criterion of effective leadership is the sort of record FDR is assumed to have compiled. On the contrary, although leadership sometimes required the semblance of achievement, it sometimes required almost the reverse.

The political dynamic of the late 1940s and 1950s differed from that of the 1930s. The postwar period may have been ill-served by an energetic presidency. FDR's formidable model of activism combined with Truman's need to appear tough produced a formula for disaster. At least Truman's decisiveness was often taken for bumptiousness or thoughtlessness. Insistently conscious of the demands of leadership in the country and in the GOP, Eisenhower behaved as if the 1950s differed from the 1930s. The critics urged that it was a case of "the bland leading the bland." But Eisenhower contended that "I don't think the people *want* to be listening to a Roosevelt sounding as if he were one of the apostles, or to the partisan yipping of a Truman." Moreover, his assistants shielded Eisenhower from many who wanted to involve the president in controversy. In contrast to Truman, Ike avoided political infighting. The lesson he took from the thirties may have been different from Truman's.

Ike considered his greatest accomplishment the restoration of the office that Truman had left in disarray. Eisenhower made little of the sign on his desk—*Suaviter in modo, fortiter in re*. It nonetheless expressed the style of governance that he was frequently taken to represent—gentle in style, firm in deed. Truman's famous sign, The Buck Stops Here, was contradicted by the inconstancy of his efforts, especially during his elected term.

Truman and Eisenhower had contrasting relations with the media. White House journalists felt a warmth for Truman, regardless of how they reported him. He hardly reciprocated this feeling (as I have suggested) because he thought his low standing with the public was caused by the press's treatment of him, a treatment he followed assiduously. Ike, however, hardly read the papers, and his interaction with reporters, though not uncordial, was distant. Newsmen did not like him even in the way they had liked Truman, and there is little evidence of mutual respect. Liberal critics poked fun at Ike's press conferences in which the president would snarl himself up in words, unable to formulate an intelligible sentence. Critics did not realize, however, that Eisenhower rarely created problems for himself in his public utterances. He may even have deliberately used his syntax to "confuse" newsmen. On the other hand, reporters at Truman press conferences seized on Truman's proclivity to shoot off his mouth. The desire to be candid made Truman look vacillating when he later shifted position, because initially he could not restrain his need for directness. Eisenhower was usually more above the battle.

The role of the media in shaping the "image" of these presidents was peripheral, as was the role of presidential "media men." Ike's message (and later JFK's) came through, whereas Truman's (and later Johnson's) did not. Or, rather, all of these men revealed themselves through the media. The electorate saw that Eisenhower had authority and that Truman did not; the voters grasped the persona of the leader, irrespective of the "manipulation" to which the journalistic community, television, or public relations specialist subjected them.

In an instructive triumph toward the end of his time in office, Eisenhower avoided the stigma of corruption that had tarnished Truman. The conduct of various of Truman's aides had damaged the president himself, but one careful student of conflicts of interest during the Eisenhower administration has contended that a series of GOP scandals was at least as serious as the ones that wounded Truman. Nonetheless, even when Sherman Adams, Ike's closest adviser, resigned under fire after charges of corruption had been made, Eisenhower escaped any taint. Both Truman and Eisenhower were protective of their associates, and like Truman, Eisenhower did not appreciate the way Adams's behavior might look. But Ike's authority was such that Adams's troubles did not rub off on him. People did simply just "like Ike" and would not believe ill of him, just as they disliked Truman and would believe anything of him.

Eisenhower made John Foster Dulles his spokesman in international affairs, and Dulles often took the heat for his chief. Dulles, however, was subordinate to the president. Although the secretary displayed the rigidity demanded by Congressional Republicans, he also pursued modest initiatives. Truman's Secretary of State, Dean Acheson, had ministered to his president's sensibilities, and he had led Truman to believe he was in charge. Truman, said Acheson, was "the captain with a mighty heart," the secretary merely his servant. But Truman grasped foreign affairs with little subtlety and, secure in Acheson's tutelage, let the State Department lead. When creative intelligence was demanded, as during the Korean War, Truman let matters drift, eventually allowing and inveigling MacArthur to involve the United States with China and failing for months to rein in the general.

Acheson could not deal with Congress. His failure to attract legislative support meant that foreign affairs in the late forties and early fifties were inevitably nasty. Under Acheson, deception became a standard ploy in presenting national security matters to Congress. On the other hand, Dulles carefully consulted Congress, and the administration's foreign policy received widespread support in the legislature.

Defenders of Eisenhower and critics of Truman have transformed these observations into evaluations of policy. In allowing Acheson's Protestant self-righteousness free expression in deeds, the critics say, Truman militarized the policy that Eisenhower later curbed. Ike's farewell address, some scholars add, warned the nation about the military-industrial complex that Truman and Acheson had done so much to create. For eight years, too, Eisenhower damped down the lust for intervention that had been brought on by the attitudes of internationalist Democrats. Eisenhower was an activist president, it has been argued, but he used power wisely and well. Democratic ideals took us into Vietnam; Eisenhower would not have.

The issue, however, should not be the disputable one concerning the comparative desirability of the Truman and Eisenhower programs. The gap between Dulles's rhetoric and the reality of his policies may have equaled that of Acheson. Ike's strategies may have been as belligerent as Truman's, and Eisenhower may have blundered as often. And so, on this view, liberal historians may be warranted in dismissing criticisms of Truman and in urging that Eisenhower's flabbiness contrasts unfortunately to Truman's toughness. The analysis of such arguable propositions, however, is important only to the debates of scholars.

The political fabrication of the meaning of events at the time was critical, and to understand this fabrication we need to see how different modes of leadership worked with the electorate and with the consistent rhythms of the electorate's emotional life. The public did not appreciate Truman's pugnaciousness. Ike may have been a doer, but that trait was inconsequential to his success with the people, just as his supposed failures were inconsequential in this respect. In a disordered period, he believed that politics was not solving problems but seeking agreement through consensus and minimizing discord. He even conducted himself as if problems did not exist. He surely did not display combative virtues or express a political vision that galvanized reflective Americans. More clearly than his predecessor, however, he orchestrated in the people the feelings they wanted to have about their president.

DURING Eisenhower's second term, liberal observers refused to give him even the half-hearted benefit of the doubt that they had accorded him in the mid-fifties. America, they said, needed direction. Eisenhower had sedated the country for too long, and the second term did look rocky to many influential commentators. As the economy lagged (in the recession of 1957–58), the management of American interests abroad—supposedly Ike's forté—seemed impaired.

In 1956 the Soviet Union put down a popular uprising in Hungary at the same time that Great Britain, France, and Israel invaded Egypt. The three powers were trying to restore Western control over the Suez Canal, seized by a nationalist regime. The United States denounced Soviet conduct, but would not endanger global stability to alter it. Simultaneously, however, American moralism, unavailing against the communists, was unleashed against the Western allies, when American influence broke the three-power sortie into Egypt. The Western alliance was shaken, the image of American invulnerability shattered.

A year later, insult was added to injury when the Soviet Union launched the first satellite. The Russian "Sputnik" apparently demonstrated that American superiority in technology did not exist, and signaled an alarming military danger. The Soviets were first into space, and, analysts worried, the Soviets also led the United States in the development of missiles and weapon systems connected to rocketry. The administration undertook a crash program. But even deeds after the fact could not counter the impression that Republicanism was sluggish and apathetic.

The contrast between Soviet dynamism and American slackness was underscored in 1960 when a spy plane was shot down over Russian territory. Eisenhower compounded the crisis by first denying US involvement. When he later admitted that an American "U–2" plane had been engaged in espionage, the public was disappointed and puzzled. It seemed that Eisenhower was not the master of his intelligence bureaucracy. Then again, some Americans wanted to know why the moral leader of the free world had sanctioned these illegal flights in the first place. Perhaps most troubling was that the Russians had knocked the plane out of the air— the intelligence-gathering seemed ineffective.

In 1960 commentators concluded that the Democrats regained the presidency because of Eisenhower's foreign policy lapses. Certainly, Ike never commanded the adulation (or the hatred) of an FDR. He was held in warm popular favor, and in the late fifties the public was made to feel a little nervous that the president—close to seventy—might not be vigorous enough to meet the challenge of the Soviet Union.

The explanation runs that the campaign between his Vice President, Richard Nixon, and Kennedy was fought over the intangibles of American prowess abroad. Ike's sway was acceptable because the electorate believed that only loose guidance was necessary. The Democrats succeeded in creating a shiver of unease that Kennedy exploited: the moral holiday had to end. The Democrat would "get the country moving again" at home and abroad. For example, Kennedy accused the Republicans— erroneously as it turned out—of having created a "missile gap" in the contest with the Soviet Union. As Eisenhower's second term ended, say the experts, Ike's foreign policy became unhinged; and so the GOP was defeated.

Nonetheless, the GOP candidate was not Eisenhower, and throughout the vicissitudes of policy that are supposed to have brought down the Republicans, the preference of the people for Eisenhower was undiminished. This continuing regard accounts for the speculation that even though his policies "failed," Ike himself could have won election again in 1960. In agreeing with other accounts, the most sober study, by Alonzo Hamby, flatly states that had Eisenhower been able to run, he could not have been defeated, and Kennedy thought that he could not have beaten Ike. Moreover, although Eisenhower was anxious to defend his administration in 1960, he had a difficult time bringing himself to support Nixon, and Nixon wanted so much to win on his own that he kept Ike out of the campaign until the last minute. Even so the vice president barely lost, and no one defeated Eisenhower.

The campaign also evidenced the continued rise in importance of TV in politics. In his controlled appearances, Eisenhower had proven himself effective in the early days of poor reception and the small black-and-white screen; McCarthy had been destroyed by TV in the famous hearings of 1954, where the senator had come across as a hectoring bully. Nixon's claim to the presidency rested on his experience in comparison to a younger and untried Democrat, and four televized presidential debates were supposed to confirm Nixon's magisterial command. In 1952, indeed, Nixon had seemed to master the new medium. In a famous speech that contained a reference to his dog Checkers, he had rebutted charges of a private campaign fund and kept himself on the GOP ticket. This performance was poltical soap opera of a high order. Republicans hoped Nixon could duplicate it in 1960.

The crucial first debate broke these dreams. The fact that Kennedy appeared as an equal in the same arena diminished Nixon. More important, capitalizing on the experiences of Nixon, McCarthy, and Eisenhower, Kennedy turned out to be a king of television, now with a larger and clearer picture, as FDR had been of radio. Commentators noted that a tense Nixon, on the contrary, sweated under the lights. Without the proper makeup, the vice president looked jowly, a bit seedy, as if he needed a shave. People who heard the debate on the radio thought Nixon did fine; those who saw it gave Kennedy the edge.

★ **7**
★ **Moment of Certainty:
1961 – 1963**

**O**ne year after his assassination in 1963, 65 percent of the electorate claimed to have voted for Kennedy, a
vote that would have made his victory in 1960 the greatest
landslide in American history. Yet the contest was in fact
one of the closest elections, with Kennedy receiving under
50 percent of the vote. Although slim, his victory bespoke
the continued power of the Roosevelt electoral coalition.
Even with a flimsy contender, Democrats could win if the
opposition was not a hero like Eisenhower. Indeed, the
marginal triumph may have been a defeat, because irregularities tainted the results in states that went Democratic by
slender pluralities. As president, however, Kennedy always
had high ratings in the Gallup polls, running as high as 83
percent.

How do we account for this reputation? To answer
this question we must understand JFK's wide appeal and
his concern for what he called "appearance."

Kennedy's informality and the attractiveness of his
wife and children were irresistible. Many women thought
of him not as a father but as a lover. For Roman Catholics,
he was above all a glamorously respectable co-religionist in
office after the tatty career of Joseph McCarthy. For the

**7. Dwight Eisenhower and John Kennedy at Kennedy's inauguration, January 1961. Chief Justice Earl Warren is behind them.**

generation of men who had fought in World War II and who had just reached maturity, Kennedy was one of them. More important, the critical group of articulate shapers of opinion, the writers and intellectuals, also found in Kennedy someone with whom they could identify. Indulging in collective self-flattery, they saw in him values they ascribed to themselves. Kennedy passed muster as a serious writer. He was the author of two popular historical works. *Why England Slept* was a study of the British appeasement of Hitler; and *Profiles in Courage* was a series of vignettes of American statesmen. Kennedy also cultivated the journalistic and artistic establishments. The nation's leadership, he believed, should be guided by a sensitive elite. Educated at the best schools and raised with a sense of *noblesse oblige* and the heritage of Western values, this elite would accept responsibility as a collective trustee for the country.

JFK's ideal was the gladiator-scholar who combined

brains and practicality. The White House entourage—the officials of Kennedy's "New Frontier"—included Rhodes scholars, professors, and historians. In theory they read and wrote, but did not restrict themselves to the cloister. Urbane and cosmopolitan, they were yet virile men of mind; touch-football was their game. Shrewdly assessing the intelligentsia's self-image, the administration gave birth to a series of clichés describing a new managerial class. It was composed of hard-nosed, tough-minded, political realists; dispassionate dissectors of ideas; can-do liberals and crisis managers with professional knowhow and expertise.

American problems, said JFK, were "technical" and "administrative," and they could be solved using the "sophisticated judgments" of this new class. Life was unfair, said this president, but we must persevere, embued with a courage that was without illusions and buoyed up by the modest hope that intelligence could minimally alter the world.

In the early years of the Depression, Hoover's technocratic intelligence was dismissed, and five years after Kennedy's death, such intelligence, personified by the men around Lyndon Johnson, was met with contempt. But in the early sixties, Kennedy struck exactly the right note about the need for expertise and the possibility of incremental social engineering. The "eggheads" of the 1950s, once they could be associated with muscularity, became culture heroes to a small but significant element of the public.

Makers of opinion were also drawn to Kennedy's self-deprecating wit and wider sense of style. As one newsman put it, "He charmed the birds out of the trees." Rejecting the idea that democracy and good taste were antithetical, Kennedy popularized high culture without making it vulgar. The poet Robert Frost contributed to the inaugural. Cellist Pablo Casals, composer Igor Stravinsky, and actor Ralph Richardson came to state dinners. The White House entertained Nobel Prize winners. Kennedy's wife was an impeccable arbiter of fashion, presiding over the entrance of the bouffant hairdo into American life, even as her husband saw out the crew cut, the male hairstyle of the 1950s. Jacqueline Kennedy's taste even extended to the striking planning of her husband's funeral.

Kennedy's understated wit soon became a staple of upper-middle-class cocktail party conversations. Entertaining the Nobel laureates, he said that this was "the most extraordinary collection of talent" ever assembled at the White House—"with the possible exception of when Thomas Jefferson dined alone." A short time later at a similar gathering, Kennedy quipped that the White House "is becoming a sort of eating place for artists." How had he become a war hero, he was asked? "It was involuntary. They sank my boat." He joked that he had appointed his brother Robert attorney general to give him "a little experience before he goes out to practice law." And after his wife had charmed Charles DeGaulle on a state visit, he introduced himself to a French audience as "the man who accompanied Jacqueline Kennedy to Paris."

The essence of the Kennedy appeal for many people lay in his success in wielding what he saw as "appearances." He consciously played on the *amour-propre* of the cultured classes. This trait, however, did not simply mark hypocrisy. Kennedy did not exude charm merely to manipulate. Rather, he believed that "appearances contribute to reality" and were central to politics.

Scholars have agreed that Kennedy was hardly an intellectual himself. His books were superficial productions and largely ghost-written. He enjoyed golf and the music of rock singer Chubby Checker. Nonethess, he recognized that it was important at the time to seem committed to the life of the mind and of the arts. Aware of the significance of the nascent civil rights movement, he placed Negroes in the Coast Guard honor contingents at the inaugural and in ceremonial military units. The president knew how these units would look to the international diplomatic corps, especially that of the underdeveloped world. He accelerated the space program because of its symbolic value. A man from the United States had to get to the moon. Why? Why climb Mt. Everest, asked Kennedy. Why fly the Atlantic alone? Why, he said speaking in Houston, did Rice play Texas? Americans undertook tasks like these because they marked significant human endeavor; not because they were easy, but because they were hard.

In April of 1962, Kennedy turned the full power of the federal government on Roger Blough of U.S. Steel to force his company to rescind a price increase. The increase, Washington urged, was unjustified. But other motives moved Kennedy: the White House learned of Blough's decision through a press release, and this treatment, Kennedy thought, defied his office. The president would not tolerate such a personal insult. For JFK the presidency represented the nation, and its eminence could not be sullied.

KENNEDY had helped to coax the public into believing that in foreign affairs America was somehow a little behind in the late 1950s. In the early 1960s he sincerely warned of crisis again and again. Scholars have disputed the wisdom of his words and the actions that accompanied them; but the president repeatedly got on the same wavelength as the citizenry. He believed that neither he nor his countrymen would exchange their watch on the bridge of liberty with "any other generation" in the history of the earth. America was the "chief defender" of freedom when it was under attack all over the globe; we were challenged on every continent. "Each day we draw near to the hour of maximum danger. . . . The news will be worse before it is better." As the president said in the inaugural speech that inspired millions, the United States would willingly "pay any price" and "bear any burden" for its ideals. He welcomed the opportunity to defend freedom in its "hour of maximum danger." "We do not want to fight," said the president, "but we have fought before." JFK's palaver suited the confident mood of the nation.

Kennedy's whole conception of foreign policy was implicated in each individual diplomatic endeavor, because each was fraught with the utmost symbolic portent. Conflicts between nations were formal contests of will in which the issue was pride. Reality indeed seemed to be tyrannized by Kennedy's "appearance." In the summer of 1961 the president returned from Vienna after a bruising discussion with Russian leader Nikita Khrushchev. "If Khrushchev wants to rub my nose in the dirt, it's all over," he declared. JFK was convinced for a time that the USSR wanted to force the West out of Berlin. The divided city was strategically unimportant, but it was an emblem of freedom in the heart of the Soviet sphere. To show his resolve Kennedy called for the building of fallout shelters. The United States would ready itself for nuclear war to protect this emblem. The president additionally resumed atmospheric atomic tests that had been previously suspended. These tests had little value, but Kennedy had to show that America would go to the limit. "I hear it said that West Berlin is militarily untenable," he commented; and so, in fact, were Stalingrad and Bastogne. "Any dangerous spot is tenable if men—brave men—will make it so." Berlin was "the great testing place of Western courage and will."

In October of 1962 the Cuban missile crisis brought out most clearly this aspect of JFK's temperament. In securing the removal of the Soviet missiles, Kennedy made the event a measure of Russian and American fortitude. The missiles were dismantled, but Kennedy, his protest to the contrary, had them removed in such a way that Khrushchev was publicly humiliated.

At one point in the tense series of exchanges, the Russians offered to dismantle the Cuban missiles if Americans dismantled obsolete missiles in Turkey trained against the USSR. Because the Turkish missiles were obsolete, the Americans would lose nothing by such a deal: the Russians would liquidate what Kennedy told Americans was a real danger in Cuba; the Americans would destroy what they believed to be superfluous missile sites in Turkey. Kennedy considered but refused such a complete victory because he thought it would look like a swap. The Russians were then given private assurances that the Turkish missiles would be removed once the crisis was over. The public response, nonetheless, had to be uncompromising. The United States went "eyeball to eyeball" with the USSR, said Secretary of State Dean Rusk. The idea was to get "the other fellow" to blink first.

In the wake of the missile crisis, the president's popularity soared, and Democrats overcame the GOP challenge at the polls in November 1962. Kennedy regularly used a language of machismo to describe the world. Indecision was effeminate; the domination of others was sexual; public conflict was about virility. This vision of things most dramatically carried over into the outcome of the missile crisis. Kennedy's confidant Arthur Schlesinger, Jr., expressed the almost erotic thrill intellectuals got from the missile crisis. The combination "of toughness and restraint, of will, nerve, and wisdom, so brilliantly controlled, so matchlessly calibrated . . . dazzled the world."

KENNEDY's belief in the importance of "appearance" is best analyzed as his awareness that the presentation of his self was indistinguishable from the state of his office. The measure of the success of the presidency was how well he came across. Consequently, he was concerned to negotiate the public's response to him, and felt the mastery of his "appearances" to be crucial. One story went that Kennedy was chided by his aides for taking an inordinate time combing his hair as he prepared to disembark from Air Force One. "It's not John Kennedy getting off this plane," he said. "It's the United States of America." The apocryphal, but public, nature of this story also suggests that people accepted JFK as he presented himself.

Some historians have interpreted Kennedy without complexity and have assumed that he was a mere manager of "appearances," a skillful opportunist. Such a view has led all commentators to propound wrongheaded questions, which have dominated American comprehension of the early sixties. These questions illustrate misconceptions about the nature of politics in the period from 1929 to 1974. Was there, historians ask, substance behind the style? Was there integrity beyond the glitter?

Historians assume that judgments about political merit must be based on true achievement or at least on a decent intention to accomplish worthwhile goals. One problem with this conception, as I have repeatedly argued, is that no one can determine what achievements are true or worthwhile. Confronted with Kennedy's magnificent command of what looks to be the genuine and worthwhile, historians assume that in examining his time in office they have an especially difficult problem in distinguishing the semblance of the good from the genuine article. They agonize about how to discover the real thing under JFK, or conclude that the president was a sort of poseur. This approach is misguided. Political achievement is not a set of characters waiting to be found by researchers or dependent upon the elucidation of evidence. Attainments cannot be discovered; they emerge in the intercourse historians have with leaders. The achievements some historians find in the early sixties and that others disparage are a product of their own idiosyncrasies and not what occurred "out there."

The feelings of the people at the time were also the

product of interaction with JFK's leadership; this interaction, however, was that of a mass public and was contemporaneous with this leadership. These feelings, it seems to me, are more worthy of investigation than the later conflicting prejudices of a tiny number of experts.

The wrongheaded concern for the possible performance behind the promise is, of course, connected with the abrupt termination of the Kennedy period and what came after it. The murder of the president and the subsequent history of the decade led to the propounding of a related question of equally dubious status that haunted the people and their leaders: what would have happened if he had lived?

It is impossible to recreate the horror and shock brought about by the assassination. Kennedy's funeral on television at the end of November 1963 was the largest simultaneous experience in the history of the human race, a final tribute to his success with that medium, and a momentous technological communion. For many people the subsequent evils of the 1960s and 1970s—war, racism, domestic violence, and political deceit—all flowed from this single senseless deed. As one poet wrote, "More than a president is dead; / And not ten thousand bullets / in ten thousand heads / could make the moment different."

In his three years Kennedy convinced people that all was in capable hands. After his death the populace felt that had he lived, the world would have continued to be intelligible and stable. Pollsters indeed showed that doubts about public life grew for almost twenty years after Kennedy's death. The persistent disgust explained why the New Frontier became a golden age. In the words of his only surviving brother, Edward, twenty years after the assassination, John Kennedy had been "made a legend."

Those who followed Kennedy vainly tried to persuade

the electorate that it could define its collective existence in other than privatized terms. Political leadership should cure what was considered a spiritual malaise. The dilemma of politicians was underscored by their monomania about Kennedy and, even more, with his family.

The Democratic convention of 1964 paid tribute to JFK, and his brother Robert participated by quoting Shakespeare:

> When he shall die
> Take him and cut him out in little stars
> And he will make the face of Heaven so fine
> That all the world will be in love with night
> And pay no worship to the garish sun.

Robert Kennedy himself was shaken by the tumultuous response to the tribute, and Lyndon Johnson hated knowing that even in tendering the presidential nomination to him, the delegates reserved their affection and even their love for the fallen leader and his family.

LBJ's inferiority about the Kennedys and "the Harvards" who ran the Vietnam war for him was well known, and Johnson's growing hatred of Robert Kennedy, who had been elected senator from New York after leaving the attorney generalship, was psychologically strategic to LBJ's commitment in Vietnam in the middle sixties. Johnson believed that he was carrying on the policy of his predecessor. He dreaded that, should his commitment falter, Robert Kennedy would rise in the Senate to denounce the man betraying his dead brother's anticommunist legacy. When Robert Kennedy did denounce administration policy, Johnson felt that nothing he could do would permit him to escape unflattering comparison to Jack Kennedy. "The thing I feared from the first day of my Presidency was actually coming true. Robert Kennedy had openly announced his intentions to reclaim the throne in the memory of his brother. And the American people, swayed by the magic of the name, were dancing in the streets. The whole situation was unbearable to me." When LBJ chose not to run for a second term, he surely had in mind the danger not merely of losing but also of having Robert Kennedy deny him the nomination.

Like Johnson, other leaders were preoccupied by the idea that the Kennedys could mobilize opinion through the story of their heroic and tragic fortunes and through JFK's claim on the conscience of the republic. The Kennedys were a royal family, deserving of an epic tale, and able themselves to mold the English language to relate it. In April of 1968, a few months before his own murder, Robert Kennedy took on the grim task of telling the residents of a black slum in Indianapolis that Martin Luther King was dead. Kennedy said that he understood their hatred and distrust because he had felt the same way when "a member of my family" was killed by a white man. Helping the crowd through an awful moment, he said Greek tragedy had taught him that wisdom came only through suffering. No other politician could quote Aeschylus in a black ghetto. No other statesman could so nobly use a grievous personal loss for his own benefit.

Shortly thereafter, at Robert Kennedy's funeral, Edward Kennedy did for the country what Robert Kennedy had done for that Indianapolis audience and expressed the hope of a family and of a nation. Elevating Robert Kennedy to the rank of the dead Kennedy president, the last son said: "My brother need not be idealized or enlarged in death beyond what he was in life. He should be remembered simply as a good and decent man who saw wrong and tried to right it, saw suffering and tried to heal it, saw war and tried to stop it." What Robert wished for others, Edward went on, the family prayed would some day come to pass for all the world. And quoting a favorite line of Robert's, he concluded: "Some men see things as they are and say, why? I dream things that never were and say, why not?"

The death of Robert Kennedy must have freed Johnson from a deep psychic burden. But the real benefactor was Richard Nixon. Nixon had to know that the second murder in the family perhaps saved him from another defeat at the hands of a Kennedy. Even this death, however, did not exorcise the Kennedy demons from Nixon. He could not drive from his mind an image of JFK that he frantically tried to emulate—even having himself photographed, in the style of the Kennedys, meditating on an ocean beach. Nixon was made furious by the knowledge that his attempts were parody; but he could not stop. Despite his anger at liberalism, the Democratic style consumed him. His speeches abounded with awkward phrasemaking in the tone of the New Frontier, haunted by a second-hand quality.

During the early 1960s and later the Kennedy administration was identified with the popular Broadway musical, "Camelot," the story of the reign of King Arthur. The tale of Camelot told of the noble king who was slain by a treacherous enemy and promised to return and deliver his people. The heart of the Arthurian legend is that the spirit of the one true monarch still wanders the land. Subsequent kings are interlopers or imposters. To deny the legend is to say that what happened after the assassination was our own fault; to accept it is to believe that what occurred was a cruel aberration and would not have happened if Kennedy or his rightful heirs—certainly his brother Robert—had been in office.

Television later made this sense of things credible. In Kennedy's death the electorate found its aspiration. The assassination and Vietnam forever severed the public from the New Frontier, but Kennedy's memory was a measure of both American desire and American despair. In the twenty-five years after his presidency, the repeated presentation of TV dramas featuring him and various members of his family testified to the president's growing, though ever altering, image. Serious critics have rightly, in one sense, dismissed these productions as "mythmaking." In another sense, however, this dismissal is a misapprehension. The television shows were a mass ritual. In the repetition of familiar events (or the introduction to them)—the inaugural address, the missile crisis, the march on Washington, the assassination—a great audience regained access to a shared past that expressed a tragic but compelling story. The audience was comforted by having the standard lines repeated again and again. Commentators have noted that the distortions in the dramas conformed to varying political biases current at any given time, but these distortions also suggest that the function of the dramas for many people was to provide solace for a world gone wrong. The message was clear. The world would be as we would like it to be now if only the president—if only his brother—had not been killed. The Kennedy shows were a species of mythmaking of the kind that also occurs in "primitive," nonliterate societies through the techniques of oral tradition. What is peculiar is that, with the subject so close in time, a technologically advanced medium created the same sort of phenomenon in the industrial West.

For the American people, the Kennedy years meant youth, purpose, talent, energy. Even though that image might become tarnished, the myth did not die. Two decades after the assassination the public, perhaps remembering that feeling of promise, ranked Kennedy as the greatest president, above FDR, Lincoln, and Washington.

LIBERAL commentators were initially inspired to contrast Kennedy's foreign policy with that which led to the Vietnam War. But Kennedy's and Johnson's "decade of disillusionment" put liberals on the run, as LBJ's troubles were linked to JFK. His supporters, William Chafe writes, "continued to argue that the president, had he lived, would never have tolerated" the war in Vietnam. But leftist and conservative critics of Kennedy have replied that the symbols he used so well were manipulated, or that, in any event, nothing lay behind them. Kennedy's incremental involvement in Vietnam, the critics add, did not differ from the strategy followed by his successor. "Vietnam," writes Frederick Siegal, "was Kennedy's legacy." Had Kennedy lived, he would have been ravaged by the war just as Johnson was. While Richard J. Walton eschews speculation, he writes that Kennedy "began the Vietnam war. It has been his most enduring legacy." There is, he says, "scanty evidence" that JFK "would not have let" American intervention go as far as Johnson did. And Bruce Miroff adds that Johnson "was only carrying on what John Kennedy had begun." From the conservative side, Fred I. Greenstein says that although Kennedy was more popular than Eisenhower, JFK did not have "to face the cost" of his commitment in Vietnam; Kennedy's decisions "might have profited" from Eisenhower's formula for decision making. The liberal response from Herbert Parmet is that "memories are notoriously short." Kennedy was ambivalent about foreign affairs, both belligerent and conciliatory. But who was not belligerent in his time? Anyone other than JFK, says Parmet, "would have been" even more belligerent. Kennedy's record was promising, states Dewey W. Grantham, and had he served a second term, there was "at least a chance" that "contemporary American history would have been considerably different." Who knows? Rather than engage in any of these conventional speculations, one could just as easily argue that Kennedy's mastery of the language through which American conduct was perceived would have transformed the experience of Vietnam and made it positive, or that under him the administration would have rolled back communism and satisfied the electorate.

The "insubstantiality" of the New Frontier could count against it only if one assumes that politics was in any way about the triumph of policies. The similarity—or dissimilarity—between Kennedy's diplomacy and Johnson's has only been crucial because historians have assumed that policies, and the Vietnam War, have an objective character. The work of Johnson and Nixon is inevitably conceived against the background of what John or Robert Kennedy would have done. This conception suggests both the president's sustained victories with the electorate in office and the impossibility of judgment. The question that haunted those who came after Kennedy cannot be answered: what would have happened, in the nation and abroad, had he remained in office until January of 1969? From the perspective of history, the president was favored, as Tacitus wrote, not only in the splendor of his life but in the opportune moment of his death. Kennedy is shrouded by the darkness of what he came to mean. He stands in the shadow of a great name.

The moral to be drawn from these facts is not that appearances were all that was potent in politics. Rather, the moral is that it is an error to search for any objective character to political performance. This is the search that entails answering questions about what policies would have been carried out in a longer Kennedy administration. Our political history from 1929 to 1974 is not epistemologically equipped to answer such queries. There is nothing more to the early sixties than what the people found there.

# ★ 8
## ★ "Let Us Reason Together"

The historiography of the decade from 1964 to 1974 resists easy classification. The most important reason for this fact is that the period is so close to us in time: comparatively few scholarly studies exist. But, in addition, Vietnam and Watergate have stymied scholars who have studied presidential history. "Johnson's war" has embarrassed liberal historians and called into question Democratic domestic policy. The scandals of the Nixon era, however, have equally embarrassed conservative commentators. Only the left has found the decade unperplexing—the period is seen as further evidence of the failure of mainstream politics. Although the more general perplexities becloud easy categorization of different appraisals of the era, these differences—and conflicting "would have" statements—still exist. This chapter and the next touch on these appraisals but concentrate on the contemporary political interchange.

In 1968 the interchange focused on Lyndon Johnson's weakness as a leader. The public reached a consensus with more dispatch than historians have been able to do thereaf-

**8. Lyndon and
Ladybird Johnson,
John Kennedy.**

ter. The people's visceral distaste for the president was
ironic: a product of his extraordinary attempt to attain the
goals liberals had promulgated for three decades.

Johnson exuded a love of getting things done. By temperament he was more aggressive than his predecessors
and he was a saavy operator. Some historians have argued,
however, that a growing commitment to liberal principles
matched his love of power and astuteness as a tactician.
Born and raised in rural Texas, LBJ was painfully conscious of regional and cultural differences and the way
they structured the rewards a person received. The inferiority he felt to Kennedy's Harvard entourage was palpable.

Concerned for the poor and disadvantaged, Johnson ad-
hered to Southern racial policies while he was a legislator as
a matter of survival. When he became vice president and
then president, some scholars have suggested, his true colors began to show.

Johnson's evolution as a statesman committed to social
justice was coterminious with the development of issues of
equality. Having picked up momentum from the late forties, the "civil rights movement" was restrained, even
genteely middle class, and its goals were first largely restricted to the south. Gaining voting rights for Negroes
there and the formal end of segregation were important
ends. Yet they were also regarded as the first steps in
achieving more substantive but vaguely defined goals of
social and economic justice. During the Kennedy era there
were many confrontations in the south over race and much
violence, or so it seemed at the time. But it appeared that
politics could contain the civil rights revolution, and that its
initial ends would be achieved peaceably.

Johnson watched these developments cautiously from
the time he entered the Senate. Disturbed by the disruption of custom, he was also disturbed by inequality. He
viewed rabid southern racist attitudes with distaste, and
he believed that the south disgraced itself by its disregard
for justice and national law. Yet he was also unwilling to
risk his career by speaking out.

By the early 1960s the pace of civil rights liberalism
quickened. As vice president, Johnson represented the electorate across the country, and he was associated with the
ornamental triumphs of the Kennedy administration. In
retrospect these came to fruition in August of 1963 with a
"March on Washington," participated in by two hundred
thousand people. Martin Luther King's oration on that
occasion intimated that racial strife would be ended, and
ended with civility. The day would come when "black men
and white men, Jews and Gentiles, Protestants and Catho-

lics" would be "Free at last! Free at last! Thank God almighty, we are free at last!" Liberals believed in legal equality but also that some benign form of social integration in both the north and the south would ultimately occur.

Between the Kennedy assassination in November 1963 and November 1964, Johnson established his own record to run for the presidency. His legislative talents, scholars have acknowledged, were superior to those of JFK, and, they have argued, secured more than Kennedy would have. LBJ combined ruthlessness and prodigious energy with disciplined commitment. His zeal to achieve racial equality coexisted with shrewd calculation. In 1964 a new civil rights act became law. It was stronger than that planned by Kennedy, and historians have argued that the murdered president might not have been able to steer such a bill through Congress. Johnson employed the memory of JFK to push the legislation through—it was a tribute to the fallen leader. The act, and one the year following, outlawed discrimination in public places and guaranteed Negroes the right to vote. As president, Johnson had matured into a champion of social justice. The 1964 and 1965 bills, he hoped, would begin to change society in the direction contemplated by the reformers who had converged on Washington in August 1963.

This legislation, I believe, is the single exception to my view that analyzing achievement is subjective. Historians try to gauge achievement by estimating the consequences of policies and gauging responsibility for the policies. In other cases they strenuously disagree, and the conflict of their evaluations belies objectivity. All observers, however, have found that politicians were instrumental in securing the goals of the early civil rights movement, legal equality and voting rights for Negroes in the south. Historians are also unanimous that these changes have been good. But this accomplishment actually corroborates my thesis about American politics from 1929 to 1974. In 1954 the Supreme

Court outlawed segregation in Brown vs. Board of Education. The court implied that formal integration in the south would be of psychological aid to Negroes. That is, what was to be gained from integration was not a material benefit but a psychic one, a spiritual gain rather than, for example, an economic one. Moreover, extending the franchise enabled Negroes to help to choose the political leadership; in my terms, to participate in the public determination of civic virtue that is central to democratic politics in the United States.

Scholars have disputed the worth of other bills that were designed to promote more substantive social justice and that, in some hazy and nonthreatening fashion, Johnson and others felt were continuous with civil rights. Typical of such legislation was the funding of the Office of Economic Opportunity (OEO) in 1964. Johnson created this umbrella agency to administer antipoverty programs. His desire to gain legal justice for Negroes ran parallel to a desire to get at the roots of injustice—the inequities that burdened millions of all races.

THE self-destructive urges of the GOP aided Johnson in his drive for the presidency. Taking over the party from the moderate and east coast Republicans for the first time since the 1930s, the right wing nominated Barry Goldwater, senator from Arizona. Goldwater was a devoted conservative, ill-adapted to rein in the ideologues who surrounded him. Galvinizing anti–New Deal sentiment, the Republican convention paid explicit tribute to Herbert Hoover. But branding Goldwater a radical who would abolish social security, Johnson spoke as one who would conserve tradition. He was acceptable to many middle-of-the-road voters who would normally have been attracted to the GOP. On the other hand, helped by his role in creating a legendary aura around Kennedy in whose steps LBJ claimed to walk, the president satisfied liberals who wanted forward-looking leadership.

Throughout 1964 fighting in Southeast Asia increased, but the conflict was not yet a major concern. In that year and the next, just as he had done on domestic issues, Johnson forged a unifying position on Vietnam with the political elite and with the electorate. At least in his speeches, Goldwater's stand on the war was more belligerent than Johnson's. The president seemed to be defending American interests responsibly; Goldwater was the war candidate.

In August of 1964 LBJ used an incident between the American and North Vietnamese navies in the Gulf of Tonkin to push a resolution through Congress authorizing all necessary military actions to protect the United States. A bombing raid retaliated against the North. Sometime in the next several months, if not then, the president decided to escalate the war. Abroad, as at home, he committed himself to large new initiatives. During the 1964 electioneering, however, he was a circumspect man of peace. On foreign as well as on domestic policy, Johnson's alliance included all but the far right.

One historian has written that a fundamental continuity of the 1960s was that it was the era of "the big promise." In his speech of 1964 outlining the "Great Society," LBJ proposed that the end of poverty and racial injustice was "just the beginning." His program would change "the meaning of our lives." "Within your lifetime powerful forces, already loosed, will take us toward a way of life beyond the realm of our experience, almost beyond the bounds of our imagination." The "best thought and the broadest knowledge from all over the world," said LBJ, would help "find . . . [the] answers for America." "We have the power to shape the civilization that we want."

The strength of the nation, the president asserted later at the Democratic convention, "is greater than the combined might of all the nations, in all the world, in all the history of this planet. And I report that our superiority is growing." LBJ's long-time friend Clark Clifford told him "this is the time to be president"; "this can be the most thrilling and the most rewarding decade in our history."

Of course, Johnson had a far greater sense of limits than some of his public utterances might otherwise indicate. He strove for "consensus" and recognized the constraints on his power. Nonetheless, he was not only enamored of a peculiar activist style but also genuinely obsessed with getting things done. For a time he convinced the people of the correctness of his ways.

In the November election LBJ won the largest popular victory in history, comparable to FDR's in 1936. The triumph was founded on the same rock: LBJ controlled the political interchange about appropriate leadership in the republic, and in that interchange the electorate was given a choice between the plausible continuation of the reasonable and the far-out. The electorate voted against Goldwater, who spoke for a long-rejected past at a time when the people exuded confidence. They were also heady with Johnson's idea that "the place is here, and the time is now."

LBJ's coattails were long, and the Congress elected at that time was the most liberal since that of 1936. Diminished conservatives could not muster enough votes to stop liberal bills. LBJ had a smashing coalition. He cloaked his purpose of raising the stakes in the battle against international communism, one part of the liberal aim. Nonetheless, the voters overwhelmingly approved his goal of social justice, the openly espoused part of the program.

The politics of 1965 was dominated by a melange of bills designed to benefit human welfare and to create his "Great Society." In addition to the Civil Rights Act of 1965, Johnson steered through a series of measures that had been defeated in the early fifties. Urban America was to be rejuvenated, and, another example of hyperbolic rhetoric, there would be a "war" on poverty.

Many critics have argued that the Great Society came to little. As the war in Vietnam drew on more and more resources, the programs ended in discord. Perhaps they were from the start a misguided dream of Lyndon Johnson and the men around him and would not have succeeded under any circumstances. More sympathetic commentators have noted that the Great Society did not evolve in an auspicious time. The tensions generated by Vietnam and the lack of money because of the war were major factors, it is claimed, in this domestic failure. Most important, intellectual energy and talent, both in the government and outside it, were consumed by the war. The United States in the late 1960s, say the scholars, would not sustain even a noble dream.

This liberal emphasis on political vision was crucial for understanding the election. In 1964 LBJ emboldened the electorate with his ideal of renewal. For a brief time after Kennedy's death, Johnson inspired the nation with hope— the hope best linked to the civil rights movement and seemingly within the grasp of liberals at the end of 1964. There can be no gainsaying the triumph of spirit that that November election brought. But a larger defeat followed this victory of faith as LBJ, like Truman before him, lost his hold on the colloquy of politics that again revolved around the terrors of communism and anticommunism.

IN the early sixties, Vietnam was only on the rim of the consciousness of policymakers. Kennedy had increased American advisers to sixteen thousand by the time of his assassination, and the difference between advising and fighting was thin. No one, however, had a plan for dealing with the possible overthrow of the south. By 1965 Johnson wanted to prevent a communist victory by wielding the military might of the United States.

Johnson was suspicious of his generals and felt uncomfortable around the "defense intellectuals" he had inherited from Kennedy. Yet, like Truman, he deferred to the foreign-policy experts. Just as Truman accepted Acheson's credentials, so Johnson accepted those of men like McNamara. And the manifestation of his patterns of inferiority and deference cost LBJ, like Truman, the support of the electorate.

LBJ was led to believe that incrementally increased destruction would cause the North Vietnamese to back down. The Americans would inflict punishment at their own discretion, and the threat of indefinitely increasing violence, so the theory went, would force the communists to leave the south. World War II had come about because the West had not stopped Hitler in the 1930s. In the 1960s the United States would prevent a third world war by halting communism in Vietnam. The tide of red domination would be turned back. LBJ would carry out the intentions of Truman, Eisenhower, and Kennedy. The fear of McCarthyism also made it appealing to fight totalitarian expansion to stave off an attack on the administration as soft on communism.

LBJ, however, could not prevail. During the sixties he suffered from the problem of credibility, or "the credibility gap." Johnson wanted to convince the people that he could take a hard line against communism and defend freedom around the world. Nonetheless, it became more and more difficult for him to maintain that what he was perceived as doing—waging a nasty war against a small adversary—corresponded to what he said he was doing. Johnson tried to overcome this tension by proving that he meant what he said: his anticommunist eloquence escalated and he became even more determined to win on the battlefield. The result was to make the "gap" even wider. "They told me that if I voted for Goldwater, we'd get into a war," one joke went. "And sure enough I voted for Goldwater, and we got into a war." The more fiercely Johnson tried to realize anticommunist ideals, the more stridently he was excoriated for hypocrisy.

The coalition Johnson had put together came apart in 1966. The center and right, at first quietly and then more noisily, made practical criticisms of the war. Each group offered reasons for decreasing the commitment, on the one hand, or enlarging it, on the other. On the left, criticism was morally vehement and came from several sources. As the fighting continued, the civil rights movement soured. Blacks demanded economic and social power, and their protests went north. Soon, blacks connected the conflict in Asia and their own plight. Johnson could not mete out racial justice while he was spending money on the war. The war, some black theorists said, was a form of racism and evidence of unwillingness to restructure society at home. Another source of disruption was the "New Left," a heterogeneous group of young people in league to stop the fighting. There was also rebellion by the "counterculture"; this collection of radicals was not in the first instance political, but it joined left-wing students in criticizing American society as war-oriented, repressive, and racist. Black revolutionaries and various white groups sided together against the "establishment." They created a climate in which LBJ's foreign and domestic policies became unhinged.

As had happened during the Truman administration, what went on abroad distortedly mirrored what occurred at home, and the president was unable to interpret events to the voters satisfactorily. A difference between the Truman and Johnson periods, however, was that in the earlier era the right had catalyzed distrust of liberals. In the 1960s they were confounded by the left.

At the time and later, many commentators dismissed the savage and unforgiving critique of the left, or explained it as a function of psychological abnormalities. The rebels of the sixties, some commentators said, were men-

144 *   Let Us Reason Together

tally diseased, similar to the right in the early fifties. The radicals were "McCarthyites of the left," and there was much to this analysis. The left's critique came to the same conclusions as did Joseph McCarthy. To the left the enemies in the 1960s were internal, liberal internationalists. At home, as if in agreement with the 1950s right, the 1960s left claimed that liberalism had not solved social problems but only succeeded in swelling the federal bureaucracy. As McCarthyites argued that Korea was an unnecessary and immoral war, sixties radicals argued that the Vietnam War was immoral and unnecessary. The sixties left, like the fifties right, had a view of America different from the liberals, and liberals attacked Joseph McCarthy and the left similarly. The left and right, liberals said, were psychically disordered; their politics could only be explained as irrationality. Perhaps, too, their activism was a function of "status" politics. Disoriented in a changing industrial order, radicals illegititmately sought in political life a solution to personal problems.

The parallels between the fifties right and the sixties left hinted that the travails of Truman and Johnson had family resemblances and that the two men were psychologically tormented in analogous ways. During the early fifties and late sixties, liberals felt anxious and not hopeful. In each period liberalism failed to evoke positive feelings from the voters. Each of these two presidents watched his authority with the electorate evaporate. Neither could prevent the opposition from shifting the axis of political interchange. During the elected terms of Truman and Johnson, liberalism was not viewed as a benignly progressive commitment, but as a seductive evil. Liberals erred, however, in stigmatizing left and right extremism as "expressive" politics; they did not recognize that all politics, their own included, was essentially expressive. At issue was not the achievement of goals but command of the moral economy.

THE protests by blacks and whites, the critiques of both domestic and foreign policy blended in a climate of brutality in the United States and in Vietnam. The warmakers in North Vietnam were aware that domestic politics could affect the formidable United States effort. At the end of January 1968, they launched a series of attacks during the Vietnamese lunar New Year holidays, the "Tet" offensive. The assault was to display enemy strength and to undermine the American will. Nonetheless, historians now agree that the north was bloodied and its fighting ability crippled for two years.

At the same time the strategy triumphed in the American mind. U.S. Commander William C. Westmoreland thought he could end the war with an infusion of some 200,000 troops in addition to the 500,000 already in Southeast Asia, and policymakers continued to talk about "the light at the end of tunnel." On their TV screens, however, Americans briefly saw the enemy in the United States Embassy itself. Focusing on what they saw, they no longer believed their military and political leaders. Respected nightly newsman Walter Cronkite told the people there would be no victory and that the United States must negotiate a settlement; the people believed television.

In the wake of Tet, respect for LBJ collapsed. The nation was preparing for November's election in which Johnson would be running for reelection. Yet the president dared to speak only at military bases; the secret service would not guarantee his safety from hostile demonstrators across the country. Bumper stickers read: "LBJ, Pull Out Now Like Your Father Should Have"; "Lee Harvey Oswald, Where Are You Now That We Need You?" Demonstrators taunted Johnson: "Hey, hey, LBJ, how many kids did you kill today?" He was almost as unpopular as Truman had been in 1952—indeed, even more so because Johnson was hated.

On March 12, 1968, Eugene McCarthy, Democratic

senator from Minnesota and hitherto a minor antiwar candidate, showed considerable strength in the New Hampshire primary. Four days later, Robert Kennedy, who had inherited the mantle of his dead brother, declared himself a candidate. As voters turned against Johnson, many rallied behind Kennedy, fostering a growing animosity between him and the president. Unlike Eugene McCarthy, Kennedy commanded the forces of Camelot and was a serious contender in the eyes of Democratic bosses. When he entered the race it was no longer clear that the president could dictate to his party. At the end of March, in personal and political agony, Johnson announced on television a limited peace move, and ended his speech by saying that he would not be a candidate for reelection. Irrespective of their positions on the war, the people cheered.

By the end of his term in early 1969, Johnson was extricating the United States from Vietnam. This reversal, which for the public coincided with Johnson's March speech on TV, came too late. An era of dissent culminated in a year of bloodshed. In early April 1968 a white man murdered revered black leader Martin Luther King in Memphis, and the most serious black rioting in the country's history followed. As Washington burned, the president readied 350,000 troops and national guardsmen to restore order. Weeks later dissident students seized Columbia University in New York City, and following their example, protestors disrupted colleges across the country. In June, two months after King's death, Robert Kennedy was shot and killed after he had won the California Democratic primary, and, many were convinced, was heading for victory at the party's August convention in Chicago.

Lurid strains in the culture were displayed in that city. Inside the convention, rule was exercised by the mayor of Chicago, Richard Daley, and by Hubert Humphrey, Johnson's vice president and now the frontrunner for the nomination. The demonstrators outside screamed for an end to war and racism. "These are our children," said *New York Times* correspondent Tom Wicker. Daley prevented live televizing of the demonstrations, but newsmen rushed to their studios with films of the activities. The television audience, in part composed of the delegates at the convention, witnessed the alternation of convention drama and urban convulsion. In what an investigating commission later termed "a police riot," the "pigs," as they were called, clubbed and beat demonstrators. In an antiwar speech at the convention, Abraham Ribicoff, a Connecticut senator of some presence, condemned "Gestapo tactics in the streets of Chicago." Daley, who had openly and uncontrollably wept at the funeral of Robert Kennedy, then told Ribicoff, in full view of the television audience, to fuck himself. The demonstrators chanted, "The whole world is watching. The whole world is watching."

Later criticism of Johnson's conduct of the war by scholarly commentators echoed the cacophony heard at the time: he should have gotten out; he should have hit the north with everything he had; he should have stayed the course. In truth, however, Johnson thought it was necessary that the electorate back him, and his policies strove to maintain consensus. In the critical winter of 1967–68, polls showed that 66 percent of the people thought LBJ was a "hawk," and 61 percent described themselves as "hawks," while 70 percent wanted to continue the bombing. Yet during this period the people's approval of Johnson fell precipitously. There are, of course, statistically consistent ways of explaining these figures, and we know that many who were opposed to Johnson wanted a stronger stand taken on the war. Nonetheless, it is more to the point to note that opinion on foreign policy was at least confused, and in any event it did not measure feeling for the president. No matter what the public thought about the war, it had become

fed up with Johnson, and to a lesser extent with Democrats. David Halberstam has written that disaffection went
"beyond ideological or partisan politics. . . . Johnson had
simply lost control of the country; there was too much
disorder; and inevitably, if unconsciously, people connected the chaos to him." Like Truman, Johnson had gotten himself into a position in which no decision he took
would be met with approval, except the decision to stop
taking decisions. Issues were not causally at work as the
electorate reacted to the person of the leader.

Newsmen and intellectuals at the time and subsequently compared the turmoil of 1968 to the Civil War, but
even with the perspective of a few years, the stability of the
system is striking. In the November election, two old pros
in American politics, Richard Nixon and Hubert Humphrey squared off. Nixon, the candidate of the center-
right, eked out a victory.

Although he was a comparatively minor figure in the
Johnson White House, Humphrey had been tarnished by
his support for the war. The vice president's "Politics of
Joy" fell victim to the rage of his progressive constituency.
He lost the election when blacks and liberals defected from
the Democratic coalition. Two strategically placed groups
vented their hostility toward the Democrats by refusing
fully to support Humphrey, for twenty years the most stal-
wart advocate of social-welfare and civil-rights liberalism,
and a man less committed to the war than his opponent
Richard Nixon. In a wider sense, too, the vote was negative. The electorate did not cast a ballot for Nixon. Angry
and frustrated, it wanted to humiliate and repudiate the
Democratic party.

WHY was Johnson such a disaster with the people? His
policy orientation was unparalleled. His unyielding commitment to an American vision of a just society was un-

matched by any other major politician in our history. In foreign affairs he tried to carry out the anticommunist ideals that had been on the lips of every important personage in politics for the preceding fifteen years.

In June of 1963 Kennedy stirred the conscience of the nation when he announced his plan for civil rights legislation. The "moral issue," he said, was "as old as the Scriptures and . . . as clear as the . . . Constitution." The same notions were given expression later that summer when Martin Luther King delivered his speech, "I Have a Dream." In the next four years Johnson tried to make this dream a reality. His addres at Howard University in June 1965 was the high water mark of the commitment to social democracy. Johnson wanted equality not just as a right or theory, but "as fact and as result." "We *shall* overcome," he said about civil rights. In Vietnam he wanted "to bring home the coonskin." "[T]here is no human power capable of forcing us from Vietnam."

Historians and political scientists have confusingly evaluated the substance of LBJ's domestic and foreign policies. Thomas Bailey and David M. Kennedy write that Johnson was a "remarkable" legislative leader on domestic issues who "crucified himself on the cross of Vietnam." Had he done nothing else in his entire life, says Doris Kearns, LBJ's contributions to civil rights "would have earned him a lasting place" in the annals of history, but in foreign policy his skills were "counterproductive." But conservative Guenter Lewy argues that American guilt over Vietnam is "not warranted." Among other things, the mobilization necessary to a victory "would have prevented" the achievements of the Great Society programs, and Lewy speculates that under other circumstances the United States "could have won" a war that had a "moral justification." At the same time, left historian William Appleman Willams laments "the visceral contradiction" at the heart of Johnson's era. The "legacy of prejudice and racism, and the global definition of America's political economy" meant that Johnson was trying "to swim in the sky" in implementing his foreign and domestic policies.

More substantial, however, than policies were feelings. Johnson did not grasp that although the voters desired the limning of a vision—an artful synthesis of thought and action—the actuality of racial justice or victory over communism was immaterial. In 1968 the nation made it impossible for Johnson to remain in the White House when he tried to make the country's moral yearnings palpable.

Liberals were brought low because Johnson mistook the ephemera of politics for its essence. Truman had legitimated a global crusade against communism. He put Democrats, especially, on the line in fighting this crusade. Then, during the Korean War Democrats came perilously close to implementing the ideals of foreign policy and, so, to war with China. For his troubles, Truman left office as the least popular president. In hindsight the message was clear: the management of ethical abstractions was significant, not the hubristic attempt to realize them. Johnson did not get the message, and his plight yields eerie evidence that there is a metaphysical difficulty to be overcome if political ideals are to be translated into the earthly realm.

To the extent that commentators have discussed LBJ's deficiencies of leadership, they have stressed his unfortunate image with the electorate. By the late sixties, when his stock was low, the media widely circulated stories of Johnson's crudity, his ego, and his petty cruelties. The president appeared as a boorish Texan, and as soon as events went against him, his inability to inspire trust or to impart dignity brought him down.

The stories varied in importance. LBJ displayed a mean streak in picking up his beagle by the ears. His vulgarity was typified when he showed off the scar from his gall bladder operation—an incident that became a famous cartoon. The president would drive around his ranch at high speeds, one hand on the wheel, the other holding a can of beer. His crassness was expressed in his delight at summoning his eastern advisers to counsel him while he was defecating. His lack of concern for the truth was apparent in his false story that his great-great-grandfather had fought at the Alamo.

The media did promote these stories—the Alamo tale was repeated even after official White House corrections. As in the cases of Truman, Eisenhower, and Kennedy, however, commentators have neglected to see that Johnson's dilemma was not a problem of image, if by "image" something duplicitous was meant. The media captured the way Johnson was. The president was vulgar, and liked raw sexual and scatological pranks. And when he tried falsely to appear as a kindly patriarch, he was universally viewed as insufferable. Torn between envy and scorn for his Ivy advisers, he was in turn self-pitying, overweening, and insensitive.

Johnson's noted troubles with the media must be connected to the kind of person he was and how the public responded to his person. This topic needs elaboration. David Halberstam related what Johnson told him he wanted from a White House aide: "I don't want loyalty. I want *loyalty*," LBJ said. "I want him to kiss my ass in Macy's window at high noon and tell me it smells like roses. I want his pecker in my pocket." What could be going on in someone's head to say this sort of thing?

The president had no sense of the role of virtue in winning friends and influencing people. He thought that the only important thing was to gain material ends for others, and thus to get their fealty. The president was not a student of history but had ardently supported FDR and the New Deal. Unfortunately, that experience fostered the specific view that the people loved Roosevelt for his achievements. LBJ wanted to be an even greater "activist" president and thus secure even greater positive support from the populace; and he would drive his staff to gain his goals. LBJ did not see that his humiliation of individuals or his deviousness or his rudeness might be of moment in his quest. The president's very success at getting things done came to contribute to the view that he was a deceitful armtwister who would do anything to get what he wanted.

By 1967 and 1968 Johnson was aware that he was hated but he could not grasp why. "How [is] it possible after all we have accomplished? How could it be?" "Deep down," said LBJ, "I knew—I simply knew—that the American people loved me. After all I had done and given to them, how could they help but love?

> I asked so little in return. Just a little thanks. Just a little appreciation. That's all. But look what I got instead. Riots in 175 cities. Looting. Burning. Shooting . . . Young people by the thousands leaving the university, marching in the streets, chanting that horrible song about how many kids I had killed that day.

JOHNSON wrongly believed that all the people wanted was the attainment of ends and a kind of largesse. In Vietnam the president was repudiated for trying to complete the task left undone by Truman. The public dismissed LBJ's domestic ideals for reasons of the same sort. Americans desired acknowledgment of and dedication to the goal of a just society, but they were leery of any real attempt to obtain it. People may have wished to hear about Martin Luther King's dream, but they did not want anyone to make it come true. Just as the electorate did not want the defeat of communism, it did not want social justice.

It will not do, here, to reply that what the people rebelled against were rather the things that accompanied these objectives—an endless war and violence and disorder at home. We live in the world, and someone who wills an end, wills the means to achieve the end. When faced with the reality of American ideals, Americans chose to deny them. The interest of the citizenry was neither social justice nor the defeat of communism. LBJ was ravaged because his concern was not the stewardship of the sacred but its attainment.

Successful presidents have coordinated the American sense of a moral community for their benefit. Because of his common misunderstanding of the New Deal and because of his personal characteristics, Johnson believed, on the contrary, that success was measured by what a president could get for "his people." The result was that "his people" came to loathe him. In alienating them, Johnson also corroborated the view that the very notion of political achievement was incoherent. When he left office, the forces interested in gaining the domestic goals of the Great Society had suffered their greatest defeat, a defeat that was perhaps mortal. When the war ended in 1975, North and South Vietnam, Laos, and Cambodia had all "gone communist," but no one seemed to care.

★ **9**

★ # Nixon and the
# Watergate Scandal

Richard Nixon scrambled to power in California in the late 1940s. Fighting campaigns noted for the "red baiting" that was becoming a key to preferment, he defeated Jerry Vorhees for a congressional seat in 1946 and Helen Gahagan Douglas for the Senate in 1950. He made his career by the successful pursuit of Alger Hiss, the most prominent figure ensnared in the spy trials of the late 1940s and early 1950s. A well-known man of the right by 1952, Nixon balanced the GOP ticket by appealing to Republican conservatives. His youth and background contrasted to Eisenhower's age and eastern orientation.

Despite Ike's distaste for Nixon, he was the heir apparent in 1960 and could not be denied the Republican nomination. When Kennedy beat him, many commentators thought that an especially unappealing figure had left politics. Two years later Nixon lost his race for the California governorship, and the prediction seemed belatedly borne out. He had a peculiarly acrimonious relationship with journalists, whom he believed always gave him "the shaft." After his defeat, Nixon "gave it to them in the backside" by telling them that they would no longer have him to "kick around." But Nixon was shrewder and had more staying power than his outbursts intimated. During the 1960s he courted the GOP rank-and-file and cultivated the role of an elder statesman, above many partisan battles yet still speaking for the center-right. Although considered unattractive as a person, Nixon appeared a safe and sober man during the tumultuous period of 1967 and 1968.

Democrats, and liberals in particular, hated Nixon as a characterless opportunist. But the disregard went deeper. In 1960 Kennedy put his finger on the factor that made Nixon so repellent to liberals and the media. Nixon went out as he went in, said Kennedy, with "no class." The man had no taste. Harry Truman got at the issue of character. All politicians lied, said Truman; the trouble with Nixon was that he didn't know the difference between lying and telling the truth. Nixon was, liberals believed, the perfect example of a situational man for whom momentary considerations were all, principles nothing.

Truman's epigram, however, suggested an integrity in Nixon. If he didn't know the difference between lying and telling the truth, then he could not be accused of lying. Nor was Nixon bereft of principle. In foreign affairs his anticommunism, it is true, was more profession than practice. His belief in a balance of power was typified by his trip to mainland China, his conclusion of the war in Vietnam, the relaxation of tensions with the Soviet Union, and the appointment of Henry Kissinger as national security adviser and secretary of state. Certainly, the president's room for maneuver in international affairs was greater than that of Democrats, for no one could fault his anticommunism. But in diplomacy Nixon's critics could have rightly noted an absence of conviction. He lacked the specific ethical vision of his liberal peers. Some historians have argued that it was just Nixon's unscrupulousness that made him so deft overseas. Like FDR he easily made and unmade commitments.

In domestic affairs Nixon was different. Exaggerating when linking New Dealers with communism, he nonetheless believed that the real enemy of the polity was the do-gooding eastern establishment. The president was less than an articulate political philosopher, but his career was unified by the theme that the liberals had fouled up America. In Nixon's eyes the liberals scorned the nation's ideals, the petit bourgeois ethos that had made the United States strong and free. The recurring difficulties of midcentury civilization had their locus, for Nixon, in the self-righteous moralizing of New Dealers. As critics have pointed out, his successful obsession with Hiss in the late forties was a function of Nixon's violent dislike of what he saw as liberal pretense.

It would be a mistake to interpret this dislike as having its center in a fear of world communism or of the welfare state. When Nixon was president, he did not overturn, even if he did not promote, liberal initiatives; nor did he

**9. Robert Kennedy.**

militantly confront the Soviets. Rather, Nixon's detestation of liberals was deeply personal—a reaction to their style, perceived arrogance, and elite education. Nixon was a sincere enemy of liberalism, but his animus was directed not so much against issues as against the tone that had emerged with FDR.

The period from 1960 to 1968 corroborated Nixon's views in his eyes. Although he coveted the Democratic pose of the majestic presidency, he believed that during these eight years the country had been fed on promises to end poverty, regain leadership, command outer space, eliminate ancient racial attitudes, and correct the abuses of capitalism through regulation. The truth was riot, protest, and discord. Much of the disharmony was due to the Vietnam War, again a Democratic failure. But much was produced, thought Nixon, by the distance between liberal pledges and social reality. That distance helped to make him president.

Nixon's speeches and public utterances rarely propounded ideals. Without the style of a Kennedy, he also lacked the geniality of an Eisenhower. America was a land

**10. Richard Nixon.**

of opportunity, Nixon said, mostly economic. He had made it; others could also if the liberals could be stopped from disturbing the nation's central institutions. During the scandals that terminated his administration, Nixon's plea—"I am not a crook"—evinced a genuine belief. Wrongdoing for him consisted only in crimes like stealing, and he had not taken any money. Morality was nothing more than prudent business dealing. Nixon never understood that for some influential Americans decent behavior involved a less materialistic vocabulary. And liberals never understood that Nixon saw in them a smug and blind moralism that had to be humbled.

SOME scholars have urged that Nixon as president was an innovative conservative, checked, as were most of his predecessors, by the fragmented Congress. In 1969 he proposed major welfare legislation. "The New American Revolution" included a guaranteed income level and work incentives for the poor. Yet when his proposals came to fruition in 1971, Congress rejected them. Nixon vetoed liberal measures in turn, but he remained convinced that the Democrats opposed him on partisan grounds and had no fiscally responsible alternatives. In 1973 his wrath at congressional irresponsibility and posturing resulted in an "impounding" scheme that would have cut off money allocated for liberal projects. Faced by an inflation that had become endemic to the economy by the late sixties, Congress still formulated what Nixon took to be grossly imbalanced budgets. Only impounding, he thought, could make the legislature approach problems realistically. The impasse exemplified Nixon's tribulations in molding the welfare state and his anger at a Congress that would not candidly grapple with national concerns. The liberals, Nixon thought, were destroying the republic.

The president's wrath was linked to the complaints

about his war policies, leveled by both Democrats and the student left. In 1970 John Mitchell, Nixon's attorney general and friend, began secret surveillance of radicals after the national guard had killed student protestors at Kent State University. The internal security division of the Justice Department would prevent people whom it defined as saboteurs from obstructing foreign policy. Although this initiative and others dealt with what the president called national security, Nixon and his associates went on the offensive against domestic foes. With an overdeveloped sense of its own beleaguered state, the White House established an "enemies list."

In 1971 Daniel Ellsberg, a left-liberal who had worked for the Department of Defense in the 1960s, gave the press access to a secret study of the war that he had worked on and that Robert McNamara had commissioned some years before as secretary of defense. When the "Pentagon Papers" were released, Nixon created a clandestine group called the "plumbers." Their job was to "plug" leaks endangering the security of the country. The plumbers undertook various shady "black-bag" operations including wiretapping the phones of journalists and officials giving classified information to the press.

Nixon and his entourage worked under the pressures of what they thought was required to end the Vietnam War. Their rationale was clear: extreme steps were needed to curtail the ruinous intrusions of the liberal left, which was sabotaging Nixon's program for peace. In the domain of national security it was justifiable to adopt methods that might ordinarily be condemned. As one of his entourage put it, "we were protecting the honorable peace that the president was bringing to Vietnam. . . . We were not covering up a burglary [at the Watergate Hotel], we were safeguarding world peace."

Rage goaded Nixon. The liberals, he thought, had created the dilemma from which the president was trying to extricate the United States. They had gotten the nation involved in Vietnam and brought into being the social crisis of the late sixties. Nixon's clandestine strategies were necessary because he had no other way to control their insolent and self-serving behavior, the consequences of which had been so disastrous to the country. Some commentators indeed found men like Ellsberg blindly overbearing, struggling to find a scapegoat for the hurt he believed liberals had done to the nation in the 1960s.

Harry Truman had often vented an untoward and bitter anger against his political opponents and newsmen, and his close associates had often protected him against his own worst impulses. So too Nixon. The president delivered rambling monologues to his aides about the liberals and about what sorts of moves might be made against them. He was not always coherent during these harangues, and what he said did not reflect his saner judgments. Nixon, many around him thought, was a bit of a lunatic, a "meatball." His more discreet and cautious advisers ignored these performances, or saw to it that the wilder ideas were buried. One of the president's circle, however, Charles Colson, was known for his ruthless lack of sense rather than his caution. Although the origins of what became known as the Watergate scandal are unknown, it may be that Nixon first broached with Colson what underhanded tactics might be necessary for the Republicans to learn about liberal strategies for the November election. Not comprehending that Nixon's ruminations were more therapeutic outbursts than realistic directives, Colson may have rushed to carry out his chief's bidding.

In any event Nixon's and Mitchell's ideas about Democratic treachery to the republic's ideals seeped down to lower-level officials. Displaying a lack of judgment but certain that the president had to be reelected to prevent liberalism from injuring the polity, these men acted perhaps without ultimate rational authority from Nixon but with the same goals. In June of 1972, a few months before the election, members of the Committee to Re-Elect the President, the GOP body charged with running the campaign, sponsored the burglary of the Democratic headquarters in the Watergate Hotel in Washington. A dutiful guard caught the intruders. Nixon quickly learned that members of his coterie were responsible for the break-in.

Nixon erred in failing to acknowledge at once the Re-Election Committee's responsibility and to purge the guilty. In August of 1972 he publicly sketched the problem exactly. "What really hurts in matters of this sort is not the fact that they occur, because overzealous people in campaigns do things that are wrong. What hurts is if you try to cover them up." Unfortunately, he was unable to act on this analysis when he proclaimed in the same speech that a "complete investigation" showed that no one in the White House was involved.

"Dirty tricks," as they came to be called, were common, as Nixon later incessantly pointed out. Indeed, Franklin Roosevelt had the equivalent of an "enemies list," and the notion of a "dirty tricks department" arose in the Truman era, when the earlier administration was deciding on measures to protect itself against the domestic scandals of the early fifties. And one of Truman's staffers—like Nixon Republican John Dean—became "the cleaner-upper of party operational crises." Presidents have often fired crooked employees to protect their office. Eisenhower, Johnson, and Kennedy rid themselves of officials who engaged in dubious activities and had probably implicitly sanctioned such conduct. But the agents were expendable when their deeds threatened the White House. Had Nixon fired the Re-election Committee, he might have weakened his campaign, but he could have appeared upright and cited the excesses of "overzealous" aides. Hypocrisy is the tribute vice pays to virtue.

Once Nixon had hidden GOP complicity in the burglary, he later compounded his embarrassments by lying. The "cover-up" expanded, as did Nixon's part in it, and then it came apart in the manner of a classic tragedy.

The president's decisions and the responses to them fed on one another. Secret groups like "the plumbers" existed because Nixon thought they were the only means to stop the liberals from bankrupting the nation. After the burglary Democrats and the liberal media went after Nixon with venom because they had despised him for twenty-five years. He retorted furiously because, he thought, they aimed to wound the presidency itself. Even in the short-term perspective, the scandals had a hyperbolic significance, each antagonist acting out a role in a drama. The moral ritual was akin to that which had driven Truman and then Johnson from office. If one individual could be sacrificed, the rest of the polity would be cleansed, as it vented its despair about the prospects of probity in the republic.

To end liberal subversion, the administration had entangled itself in burglary, spied on its opponents, and wiretapped their conversations. It interfered with investigations of the FBI, the Justice Department, special prosecutors, and Congress. Officials engaged in a multitude of "tricks," destroyed evidence, blackmailed each other, and perjured themselves. These activities were different in degree but not in kind from standard procedures in politics. Indeed, they were the domestic equivalent of similar pursuits overseas. By the late 1950s it had become common to use any means to best a totalitarian enemy. Surreptitious operations, lying, the falsification of records, and worse were all considered acceptable in international affairs. Arthur Schlesinger's important book *The Imperial Presidency*

(1973) makes this argument, although it exempts FDR from such means and is pervaded by liberal evaluations. Nixon's error consisted in his stumbled-footed attempts to preserve the appearance of not having done what he did. The American people, he once cagily pointed out, were like children who wanted to believe their leaders. But the president was ill-equipped to convey trust and assurance to a mass of people, and this maladaptation led to his resignation. His deeds, however, were a tenuous reason for impeaching him, as opposed to other presidents.

THROUGHOUT his political life, Nixon succeeded by ministering to the electorate's anger, as FDR sometimes had. Nixon almost seemed conscious that he would have power if he could dominate political interchange about resentment. He was astute in focusing this interchange at appropriate times—the late forties and the late sixties—on the electorate's distaste for liberals. When the people got fed up with liberals, Nixon was always around to embody their anger.

Yet this analysis is too simplified. In 1968 Nixon did appeal to frustration; but he was also concerned with forging something more than a negative coalition. He wanted to speak for the "silent majority," "the great majority," "the forgotten Americans," and in creating a consensus after his victory, he spoke of the need to "bring us together." This rhetoric of community appeared now and again thereafter, when, for example, the Kent State shootings prompted him to enter into a dialogue with angry students. Nixon's instincts, however, repeatedly suggested polarization. In the 1970 congressional campaign his rallies promoted the entree of demonstrators so that "terrorists of the far left," "a small group," a "minority" could be contrasted with the "great silent majority" for whom the president spoke. This strategy culminated in the 1972 election, when

Nixon decisively defeated George McGovern. The Democratic campaigner was inept. "I am not," said McGovern, "a 'centrist' candidate." He lent himself to Nixon's attempt, like Roosevelt's in 1936 and Johnson's in 1964, to define the race as one between the great mass of voters and a few people bent on perverting American ideals. Nixon adroitly calculated the public's hatred. When told that his only moderate position in opposition to the leftist Democrats might lose him the support of conservatives, he said, "Let them vote for McGovern."

The resentment Nixon stoked had always been directed against liberals, and he had triumphed—in the late forties and again in the period from 1968 to 1972—when hostility toward liberals was at a peak. But the motivating force in Nixon did not come and go: it was buried in his psyche and drove him incessantly. His periodic electoral victories were only the public manifestations of a persistent bitter aversion for men like Hiss and Ellsberg. This enmity finally led Nixon seriously astray. His 1972 victory was built, like FDR's comparable one in 1936, on the solid foundation of public indignation. But Roosevelt had little difficulty in turning to new areas of popular interest after lambasting selfish businessmen; he had a remarkable sense of those areas, and no inner compulsion to attack the wealthy. Nixon was incapable of such opportunism; he was incapable of changing his tune. As the Watergate affair unfolded, Nixon's inability to distance himself from his demon proved catastrophic. The contemporary master of the Rooseveltian politics of victory through polarization found himself on the wrong side of a polarized dialogue. The citizenry was asked to choose between the Constitution and the rule of law, on the one side, and the dictatorial ambitions of a single individual, on the other.

The irony of Watergate was that Nixon, who had such a rare grasp of the dialectical power of resentment and who had used it so brilliantly, was himself caught in a dialectic that could only hurt him. What led him into such a morass? Essentially, I think while the president had a sixth sense about the grievances of the citizenry when they paralleled his own, he could not at all sense when these grievances differed from his; he was deaf when the public was not aroused against liberals. His disgrace stemmed from a psychological defect: he was so contorted by his own hatred for the liberals that he could not get outside it, even when it was prudent to do so.

Once again the appropriate comparison is to Harry Truman. Like Truman, Nixon lacked an acute sense of balance between political expediency and loyalty to his inner circle and how his synthesis of expediency and loyalty looked to the public. The outcry about communist subversion successfully made against Truman at the end of his elected term was separate from the charge of corruption. But that charge was connected to the charge of usurpation of power made in the steel seizure case. Truman did not see how his support for "crooked" associates and the image of dictatorship damaged his standing. The failure of perspicacity was similar to Nixon's. Both men lacked a delicate notion of how the electorate construed their behavior. In Nixon's case, scandal, subversion, and a vision of dictatorship came together. The Supreme Court's contribution in 1974 was the citation of the steel seizure case as a precedent to Watergate in the abuse of presidential authority.

By the middle of 1973, six months after his huge victory, Nixon was in the position of Truman in 1952 and Johnson in 1968. Seventy percent of the people approved of his conduct at the beginning of his second term; a year later only 27 percent did. His reelection was a singular testimony to his success with the public. But the rapid and decisive turnaround in his fortunes demonstrated how much more significant was his incapacity to induce faith.

Nixon's defenders have argued that Watergate was not an impeachable offense and that the constitution would not have been threatened had he remained in office. His defenders add that what Nixon would have accomplished in foreign affairs had he not been dismissed from office would have overshadowed the evils of domestic corruption. For the liberals, on the contrary, Nixon was an American fascist, an unscrupulous man who had to be stopped if the constitutional system was to prevail. Had he not been stopped, the argument goes, the American system would have been destroyed. Watergate was part "of a large pattern of corruption of power . . . at the center of the Nixon presidency," and Nixon's resignation, liberals suggest, was "a vindication of the ability of the American constitutional system to right itself." But, for the left, Nixon was simply an extreme embodiment of "the system," a man who had had to go but who was not unlike many of his peers. The left suggests that the system was "inflexible" and that we were lucky that Nixon was caught; his doings were "only one episode in the seamy history" of "the secret state," "just another example of . . . corruption." Each of these views might be deepened by reflecting that Nixon—like Truman—was rehabilitated as an elder statesman.

Weighing the ethics of Watergate, however, misses the emblematic quality of the politics of the early 1970s. The main difference between Nixon and men like Kennedy and Johnson was that Nixon was believed to be uniquely offensive. He knew this himself. Reporter Dan Rather once surprisingly asked the president one of the "most popular" questions of the press corps. People gave Nixon, said Rather, high marks for decisiveness and willingness to change; but they said he "had failed to inspire confidence and faith and lacked personal warmth and compassion." "Why do you think that is?" said Rather. Nixon said ". . .that is what the people . . . believe. . . . my strong point is not rhetoric, it isn't showmanship, it isn't big promises—those things that create the glamour and excitement that people call charisma and warmth. My strong point is performance." Later, when Watergate and the liberals had brought him low, he said "I gave them a sword and they stuck it in, and they twisted it with relish."

The hysteria of the era was like that of twenty years before when Joseph McCarthy had played on the fears of the electorate to drive the Democrats from office. Democrats in the seventies also created a crisis of legitimacy. Just as the Nixon administration covered up its mistakes, so too Truman and Acheson had denigrated the charges of their critics and tried to stifle congressional investigations like those of Joseph McCarthy and the young Nixon. In 1973 and 1974, however, Nixon's enemies and not his friends authoritatively spoke out on the question of the subversion of the republic. Moreover, the critique that the liberals delivered against Nixon was similar to the one he (and McCarthy) had made of them in the late forties and early fifties. Executive privilege and secrecy were Joseph McCarthy's—and Nixon's—favorite examples of the abuse of power. In the earlier period, however, the desire of the federal government for secrecy was defended by the same sorts of people attacking clandestine activities in the executive branch in the early 1970s. One of the few men who was publicly consistent over this twenty-year period was James St. Clair. In 1954, he was a young assistant to Joseph Welch, the man who as counsel for the army during the army-McCarthy hearings denounced McCarthy and defended executive privilege. In 1974 St. Clair reappeared as Nixon's lawyer, again defending executive privilege. Finding him mildly heroic in the fifties, liberals viewed St. Clair in the seventies with distaste.

The ability of presidents to withstand assaults on their conduct, no matter how outrageous it might appear to critics, was owed in part to the successful censuring of Mc-

Carthyism in the middle fifties. For a long time attacks on executive prerogatives could be discredited by associating them with McCarthy.

The issue in both eras was the corruption of the republic. During each period charges about the perversion of their sacred ideals perplexed Americans. In the early fifties and again in the early seventies the nation found that the most insidious enemy was within. In the earlier period, people were afraid of these enemies. In the later period, they came to be delighted with a morality play in which "the good guys" would win. Each time a victim was found whose punishment would atone for the nation's falling away from its heritage. In 1950 Alger Hiss—and then Truman—played this role as the right exorcised a left-liberal demonology. In 1974 the role was Nixon's, as left-liberals exorcised the demons of the right. Just as Hiss may have been guilty but was unfairly pilloried for the supposed vices of his generation, so too a guilty Nixon was made a scapegoat for the problematic aspects of political life in the late 1960s and early seventies.

Watergate had even a larger significance for liberals. The scandals were only an example, for them, of the recklessness of Nixon's career. He had always overstepped the bounds of decency; he had always displayed the dark side of American life. Just as what Alger Hiss had done or had not done had been secondary twenty-five years earlier, so Nixon's more recent crimes were secondary for liberals. The man had to be punished. The issue was vengeance. They believed that when Nixon left office, the New Deal—battered in the early fifties and then again in the late sixties—would be somehow restored.

FDR's great victory of 1936 displayed the way a leader might benefit from his contribution to the interchange about subversion and countersubversion. In the early seventies Nixon showed how turns in that interchange might humiliate even an expert.

# ★ Conclusion

This book expounds a thesis about American politics from 1929 to 1974. I am not oblivious to the continuities between that period and the present; but as an historian my concern is not the 1980s. Nor is my concern Nazi Germany, local politics, or primitive societies, but what may be a unique time in our presidential democracy. The thesis is not intended to exemplify a general theory applicable to other cultures in other times or to other political systems. My interest is not philosophical ethics or the theory of knowledge.

From the Depression to Watergate, leadership succeeded with the citizenry when it evoked a positive emotional response; it failed when that response was negative. I have explored the sacred and dramatic aspects of this process. In 1932 and 1936 Hoover and FDR demonstrated how the emotive meaning central to politics was brought into being. Equally instructive, however, were the events of 1973–74. Just as Roosevelt's victory showed how a leader might benefit from dominating the interaction between president and public, Nixon's resignation exemplified how a leader might be harmed by being dominated by the interaction. The administrations of Eisenhower and JFK indi-

**11. *Inauguration of John Kennedy. The five past, present, and future presdents in the picture are, left to right, Eisenhower (next to Jackie Kennedy), Kennedy, Johnson, Nixon, and Truman.***

cated that dramatically different "styles" could be successful: the efficacy of the presentation of self was a function both of the self presented and the temper of the audience to which it was presented.

The contrary view—that objective appraisals of policy should determine presidential success—is vitiated by the inability of the experts to arrive at a consensus on the quality of policies. Scholars simply do not have a procedure for figuring out what would have happened if policies other than those adopted had been carried out. Nor do they know how to solve the connected problem: to demonstrate that the policies that were carried out were instrumental in bringing about certain changes—perhaps the changes would have occurred no matter what was done.

The role of policy was different from what it was usually understood to be. Truman's experience intimated the way issues were the vehicle through which presidential performance was assessed. But the difference between Truman's (and Hoover's) comparative consistency, on the one hand, and FDR's vacillations, on the other, also evidenced that fidelity to policy was no guide to electoral approval. Moreover, the doings of the Johnson administration and its undoing showed that a serious attempt to attain agreed-upon goals did not guarantee civic approbation. Finally, under Eisenhower especially, no policy orientation was supremely important, even as a medium for large-scale approval or disapproval. In general, there is no connection to be made between subsequent evaluations of the quality of a policy or the moral goodness of an issue and the feelings a leader associated with that policy or issue could generate. This fact prompts the significant conclusion that from the Depression to Watergate, the elaboration of plans did not generate mass emotion in a way amenable to what is usually understood as rational analysis.

Statesmen tried to control the responses of the citizenry by identifying themselves with the public good. But no one has agreed on what the public good in any given case was, or if the president actually fostered it. Attempts to impute pragmatic rationality to politics all founder upon this fact.

Let me make this point in another way. The response of the public to leadership was never caused by the intrinsic quality of policies—the presentation of the public good—although the response was made through salient aspects of policies. That is, the public response did not derive from its intellectual understanding of policies but from the provocation of its feelings. This provocation was the outcome of a process in which the significance of policies was not discovered but created. The essential characteristics of issues were produced in the culture and were not inherent in events.

The public at the time did not simply recognize that

FDR's conduct of World War II was "good." Nor did a later public just come to see that Johnson's conduct of the war in Vietnam was "bad." From 1939 to 1941 there was substantial opposition to American entry into the world conflict, and historians have pointed out that the cause of American entry into the war—the Japanese attack on Pearl Harbor—was not simply an evil deed. World War II became constituted as good by Roosevelt's ability to associate himself with occurrences that the citizenry, with FDR's help, invested with positive meaning.

As I have said, commentators often write that if JFK had lived, he would have removed the United States from Vietnam and saved the nation from the turmoil of the sixties. Yet during the Kennedy and early Johnson years, the Vietnam War was an effort that generated public support. Kennedy's abilities in inspiring the polity might have made Vietnam a positive endeavor. Vietnam was made bad as the people joined in a dialogue with Lyndon Johnson.

The prestige of Roosevelt and LBJ in each war was contrived, crafted in the interchange that took place between the populace and the national leadership. Students of these wars in particular, and of American history from the Depression to Watergate in general, have assumed that political events and policies had a certain nature that the people more or less dimly perceived and evaluated, and that historians and political scientists perceive less dimly and thus evaluate more clearly. The quality of these events, however, was not there: that is why later commentators so violently disagree in their judgments. Rather, expert appraisals of past politics depend on many subjective factors, chief among them—as I have pointed out previously—the connection of the expert to the transformations of the New Deal period. And for the citizenry at any time, the value of circumstances was not disclosed but came into existence in a discourse that successful politicians were able to form for their benefit.

It would be a mistake, however, to think that what counted was what politicians said and not what they did. What counted was neither what leaders said in any simple sense, nor what they did; their doings had no objectively verifiable nature, and their words were sometimes efficacious, sometimes not. What was crucial was the ability of leaders to embody whatever happened with emotions advantageous to themselves.

THE evaluations of historians are vitiated by peculiarly contestable "would have" statements. But then, it might be asked, are not all evaluations vitiated, including any that may be implicit in my own text? This is an important question that can be answered by elaborating on the two purposes of the book. First, in giving examples of the "would have" statements that scholars propose for our acceptance (and that other scholars dismiss), my purpose has been to suggest that the "would have" statements reflect a narrow range of conventional political judgments. Even if historical understanding is limited by reliance on "would have" statements, there is no need that these statements be restricted to those that embody the predictable political assumptions of a tiny group of scholars.

The other purpose of the book has been to investigate the assumptions of the people. The debatable "would have" statements tell us about the feelings of historians, when the history of our politics from 1929 to 1974 was about the mass feelings of the citizenry at the time.

Are not, however, the "would have" statements that the public believed in, if they did, or the "would have" statements on which I have implicitly relied in exploring the responses of the public just as problematic? Perhaps they are; but the purpose of the book in delineating the responses of the people has not been primarily to justify these responses but to describe how they worked themselves out. I do not know if the electorate was correct in believing that if Kennedy had lived, the experience of the United States in the late 1960s would have been positive. Would the people have responded positively to Truman if he had been president from 1941 to 1945 rather than from 1950 to 1953? Or negatively to FDR if he had been president from 1964 to 1968, instead of from 1941 to 1945? Would Hoover's or Nixon's fate have been the same had either been elected at other times? If Kennedy had been defeated in 1960, as my fantasy presumes, would he have become a figure like Nixon? I do not know.

I have been interested in the fact that certain presidents and not others gained public approbation; and I have been interested in locating a minimal pattern in these facts. But I have not tried to judge how at any time the public would have responded to different leaders, or leaders to different publics.

The point of my fable and of my emphasis on historians' "would have" statements is to sensitize the reader to the ways in which historians try to persuade their reading audience to share their feelings in the absence of compelling evidence. In examining the feelings of the people—and whatever "would have" statements are to be associated with centering attention on their feelings—my intent has been different. I have wanted to imply that a more appropriate historical task than the display of individual emotion about past presidents would be the exploration of the emotions of past electorates.

SOME readers may understand this text to be criticizing an antidemocratic bias in the work of historians, and to be defending the democratic nature of American politics. Take historians' treatments of Roosevelt, Truman, and Eisenhower. Ronald Radosh argues that "the people" responded positively to FDR because of "their own deeply held illusions"; and Paul Conkin writes that because the New Deal programs sought security for the big business system, FDR's enemies "should have been friends." According to these historians, neither Roosevelt's contemporary defenders nor his detractors showed political acumen; only historians writing after the fact can judge whom individual voters should have supported.

Or take the case of Truman. His supporters believe that Truman was a figure who showed that industrial democracy could find great leadership in a "little man." This is, however, a patronizing view of the ordinary American. During his incumbency, the public persistently believed that Truman lacked the critical talent for leadership; the people thought "the little man" a disaster. In making a hero of one ordinary man, liberal historians have had to dismiss the views of the ordinary Americans of the 1940s.

Finally, consider what liberals say of Eisenhower. Carl Degler defends FDR's leadership and denigrates Eisenhower. But although Ike commanded popular favor similar to Roosevelt's, Degler writes that Ike's monument is only likely to be inscribed, "The best-liked man ever to be President"; he will never be included in "that tiny pantheon of great leaders of Americans." Historians have faith in the electorate only when it shows the good sense to agree with them.

In looking to the people as a touchstone of what was happening in politics, this book may thus provide ammunition for a defense of democratic politics. The interpretations of the experts are politically prejudiced because of the extraordinary impact of the Roosevelt presidency. A further argument could propose that once the experts' model of achievement is discarded, so too are conventional political values. This change, however, does not mean that political understanding is value-free. Instead, the sorts of evaluations are less conventional. The values implicit in this book are those that arise from putting faith in a mass electorate and not an elite.

The people, much theorizing to the contrary, were not fickle. They responded to leadership with a fair amount of consistency. They found Herbert Hoover to be heartless, warmly embraced FDR for twelve years, and were always suspicious of Truman's competence. The people had a generous and enduring regard for Eisenhower and Kennedy. After Kennedy's death, there was bewilderment: the great electoral victories of 1964 and 1972 were not followed by further evidence that the voters had a sustained preference, respectively, for Johnson and Nixon. But it is not surprising that Vietnam and Watergate perplexed the people, and despite the perplexity the people's response was not chaotic. Johnson's quest for affection led the people to detest him, and the citizenry's respect for Nixon was always touched with a contempt that became overwhelming. These judgments may all be worthy of respect. If we believe in the principles of republican government, it is difficult to see why the conflicting estimations of a scholarly elite are to be preferred to those of the citizenry.

Part of the reason presidents triumphed was that they believed they deserved to rule and believed they were successful. FDR and JFK may have been hypocritical, though I do not intend that word to have a negative connotation, but they were confident that their reigns were meritorious. Eisenhower was no hypocrite but also had confidence in his own leadership. The people estimated these men at the value they put on themselves. Moreover, the electorate perceived the weaknesses that Hoover, Truman, Johnson, and Nixon exuded and were themselves aware of. The people felt pessimism and uncertainty in Hoover, inadequacy in Truman, desperate craving in LBJ, and deviousness and insecurity in Nixon. Much has been made of the manner in which the media controlled political image making and were themselves shaped by the attempt to present an image. But reality did not belie these judgments of the electorate. So far as we can tell, essential realities were apprehended via the media, no matter what the communications experts, in the media and of the politicians, attempted. There may be something to be said for the electorate's implicit assumption that it was better to have a president in office who had a sense of his self-worth than one who did not; and something to be said for the electorate's sense of who had and who did not have a sense of this worth.

Yet any defense of democratic politics is not intrinsic to my purpose. My notion of who the successful presidents were may be open to challenge; I can only appeal to readers to examine the various bits of evidence we have to see if the sense that historians have of the men who commanded the allegiance of the people is accurate. I can, moreover, only recall to readers what I believe to be common assumptions about the nature of our democratic politics: that preferences are comparative but that the approval of something over 50 percent of the electorate indicates a national trend. I have accepted these assumptions in this book, but have not defended them.

I do think, however, that we ought to recognize that politics in this period is to be preeminently understood as an on-going communal emotional experience. As such it is not an enterprise to be sneered at; nor is it the task of scholars to undermine it, circumvent it, or to rail against it. The initial goal should be to see how it works. We all have our feelings about the past, and about the present—indeed the two are inseparable—about what is good and bad, about what should have been done, or not done, at particular times. But our individual feelings have no absolute validity; and so, I think, the mass feelings that existed at any point in the past should be respected as facts (similar to our own present feelings) that fundamentally condition, and should condition, past political behavior. There is thus a legitimacy, for a believer in a republican civic life, to the view that politics should concentrate on how people feel, on the emotional life of the nation. Not to place that aspect of politics at the center of attention in one's historical analyses is to do violence to what politics is all about.

I have given an account of what took place in the interchange between politicians and the electorate, but my explanations of how successful presidents actually managed public moods were limited. For example, I have not even attempted the structural job of determining if there was a political class or political groups that represented or influenced critical segments of the electorate; I have merely accepted our intuitions of the moral legitimacy of the citizenry acting in concert and tried to see where it led us. Moreover, I would not claim even to have adumbrated an adequate normative criterion of what the "good ruler" should accomplish. In examining political leadership with recourse to the values of the public, we are left with far more problems than solutions.

We know that we must grasp, first of all, the dynamic of the peculiar social psychology that was critical. A crucial aspect of this psychology was the president's participation in an almost ritualistic give-and-take about what were at the time the endangered ideals of the republic. Hoover, FDR, Truman, LBJ, and Nixon were all engaged for better or worse in such a struggle. The interchange differed, although communist subversion was the focal point at many times. Under Roosevelt, however, the irresponsibility of business was central, and under Nixon the sordid dimension of public affairs itself. Nonetheless, the interchange was not always pronounced: it was more muted under Eisenhower and Kennedy than before and after their times.

Other common threads are hard to discover. Charisma, whatever it is, served FDR and JFK. Yet Eisenhower was not clearly a charismatic figure, and although his stance "above politics" worked wonders for him, the same stance was disastrous for Hoover. A technocratic emphasis also injured Hoover, but it aided Kennedy. Truman's troubles came about because he lacked authority, but Nixon and Johnson did not lack authority so much as they lacked characters that could make them appealing to the people in stressful periods.

AMERICAN politics from 1929 to 1974 was paradoxical. In that period the enterprise was a form of mumbo-jumbo; but the mumbo-jumbo was profound—it provided the framework for collective human endeavor. The belief that policy counted is an illusion. But even if it was an illusion necessary to our engagedness in our politics and our culture during those five decades, it need not be necessary to the understanding of this politics and culture.

# ★ Essay on Sources and Methods

The narrative material in this book derives from published sources, mainly the large secondary literature by historians. I have, of course, tried to be factually accurate in those parts of the book devoted to more-or-less simple storytelling, but I would appreciate having pointed out to me any errors that have occurred. More important, I have attempted to present the basic story in as uncontroversial and neutral a way as possible; but the histories I have used assume that the incorporation of their political views into political history is acceptable. I would consequentially also appreciate the pointing out of any political prejudice in the narrative. Such prejudice, however, should be peripheral to the interpretive slant of the book.

I have compiled below a very select list of sources from which I have derived my narrative. I have also provided citations for the opinions of experts I have specifically quoted and for illustrative material that is not, to my knowledge, available in the secondary literature.

ALTHOUGH there are no authoritative scholarly works that cover the fifty years of political history I have surveyed, there are many excellent textbooks in American history that elegantly recount these facts and that provide full and up-to-date bibliographies. The reader interested in examining the enormous monographic literature of recent political history is referred to any of these bibliographies. I particularly recomment the latest editions of *The Great Republic: A History of the American People* by Bernard Bailyn, et al., and of James T. Patterson, *America in the Twentieth Century.*

Surveys of certain themes in American history that raise some of the issues important to this book include: Otis Graham, *Toward the Planned Society: From Roosevelt to Nixon* (1976); William Leuchtenburg, *In the Shadow of FDR* (1983); Theodore Rosenof, *Patterns of Political Economy in America* (1983); Frederick F. Siegal, *Troubled Journey* (1984); Alonzo Hamby, *Liberalism and its Challengers* (1985); Russell L. Hanson, *The Democratic Imagination in America* (1985); William Chafe, *The Unfinished Journey* (1986); and Peri E. Arnold, *Making the Managerial Presidency: Comprehensive Reorganization Planning, 1905–1980* (1986).

On the evaluation of political leadership, see Angus Campbell, Philip E. Converse, Warren E. Miller, and Donald E. Stokes, *The American Voter* (1960); APSA, "Toward a More Responsible Two-Party System: A Report of the Committee on Political Parties, American Political Science Association," *American Political Science Review* 44 (1950): supplement, number 3, part 2; and Evron M. Kirkpatrick, "Toward a More Responsible Two Party System: Political Science, Policy Science, or Pseudo-Science?" *American Political Science Review* 65 (1971). Recent political science approaches can be found in Morris P. Fiorina, *Retrospective Voting in American National Elections* (1981).

Historians have explicitly participated in rating presidents as if the latter were students of the former. See Robert K. Murray and Tim H. Blessing, "The Presidential Performance Study: A Progress Report," *Journal of American History* 70 (1983–84). The journal *Reviews in American History* is a unique source for exploring the peculiar notions that historians have about their competence to examine national political leadership. Two brief essays are exemplary: Arthur Schlesinger, Jr., "The Ike Age Revisited" 11 (1983); and Richard T. Ruetten, "Another Look at Lyndon" 13 (1985). The attempt to connect issues to voting preference in a "rational" fashion is illustrated by Thomas G. Paterson and William J. Brophy, "October Missiles and November Elections," *Journal of American History* 73 (1986–87). Similar notions appear in works of political science. An authoritative recent source is Richard Neustadt and Ernest R. May, *Thinking in Time: The Uses of History for Decision Makers* (1986).

On leaders and their relations to the media, see James Pollard, *The Presidents and the Press* (1947), and *The Presidents and the Press, Truman to Johnson* (1964); Douglas Cater, *The Fourth Branch of Government* (1959); Elmer Cornwall, *Presidential Leadership of Public Opinion* (1965); Gene Wyckoff, *The Image Candidates: American Politics in the Age of Television* (1968); William Rivers, *The Adversaries: Politics and the Press* (1970); James David Barber, *The Presidential Character: Predicting Performance in the White House* (1972); David L. Paletz and Robert M. Entman, *Media, Power, Politics* (1981); Doris A. Graber, ed. *The President and the Public* (1982); Kathleen Jamieson, *Packaging the Presidency* (1984); Barbara Kellerman, *The Political Presidency: Practice of Leadership from Kennedy Through Reagan* (1984); Edwin Diamond and Stephen Bates, *The Spot* (1984); W. Russell Neuman, *The Paradox of Mass Politics: Knowledge and Opinion in the American Electorate* (1986); Lynda Lee Kaid, Dan Nimmo, and Keith R. Sanders, eds. *New Perspectives on Political Advertising* (1987); and Benjamin Ginsberg, *The Captive Public: How Mass Opinion Promotes State Power* (1987). See also, Graham J. White, *FDR and the Press* (1979); *Propaganda in an Open Society: The Roosevelt Administration and the Media, 1933–1941* (1985); Emmet Hughes, *The Ordeal of Power: A Political Memoir of the Eisenhower Years* (1963); Robert H. Ferrell, ed. *The Diary of James C. Hagerty: Eisenhower in Mid-Course, 1954–55* (1983); Montague Kern, Patricia W. Levering, and Ralph B. Levering, *The Kennedy Crises: The Press, the Presidency, and Foreign Policy* (1985); Pierre Salinger, *With Kennedy* (1966); Peter Braestrup, *The Big Story: How the American Press and Television Reported and Interpreted the Crisis of Tet 1968 in Vietnam and Washington*, 2 vols. (1977); Kathleen J. Turner, *Lyndon Johnson's Dual War: Vietnam and the Press* (1985); George Reedy, *The Twilight of the Presidency* (1970); Joe McGinnis, *The Selling of the President, 1968* (1968); James Keogh, *President Nixon and the Press* (1972); Ron Nessen, *It Sure Looks Different from the Inside* (1979); and Joseph Spear, *Presidents and the Press: The Nixon Legacy* (1984). An excellent bibliographical essay that covers these matters in respect to foreign affairs is William Widenor, "The Role of Electoral Politics in American Foreign Policy Formulation," *Society for Historians of American Foreign Relations, Newsletter* (December 1985). On foreign policy also consult Marian Irish and Elke Frank, *U.S. Foreign Policy: Context, Conduct, Content* (1975).

Although I have not intended to write an academic book, in framing my ideas I have been inspired by two model texts: Arno J. Mayer, *The Dynamics of Counterrevolution in Europe* (1971) and Paul K. Conkin, *The New Deal* (rev. ed., 1975). Other substantive studies have also stimulated my thinking. Most significant among these are those by Richard Hofstadter, *The American Political Tradition* (1948); Thomas C. Cochran, "The Presidential Synthesis in American History," *American Historical Review* 53 (1948); and Richard Neustadt, *Presidential Power* (1980 ed.).

### 1. THE INSPIRATIONAL PRESIDENCY

Arthur Schlesinger, Jr., associated Hoover with the "old order" in *The Age of Roosevelt*, vol. 1., *The Crisis of the Old Order, 1919–1933* (1956), while Joan Hoff Wilson wrote *Herbert Hoover, Forgotten Progressive* (1975). William E. Leuchtenburg wrote that the New Deal achieved a more just society in *Franklin D. Roosevelt and the New Deal* (1963), while Janet Poppendieck talked about the "paradox" of capitalism in *Breadlines Knee-Deep in Wheat: Food Assistance in the Great Depression* (1986). Robert Ferrell appraised Truman as one of the best presidents in *Harry S. Truman and the Modern Presidency* (1983), while Richard Freeland denigrates Truman's accomplishments in *The Truman Doctrine and the Origins of McCarthyism* (1972, 1985).

Herbert Hoover's own writings are the best place to get a glimpse of him: *Principles of Mining* (1909); *De Re Metallica,* trans. by Georgius Agricola with Lou Henry Hoover, with an introduction (1912); *American Individualism* (1922); *The Challenge to Liberty* (1934); and *Memoirs,* 3 vols. (1951–52). William E. Akin, *Technology and the American Dream* (1977); Craig Lloyd, *Aggressive Introvert: Herbert Hoover and Public Relations Management, 1912–1932* (1972); William J. Barker, *From New Era to New Deal: Herbert Hoover, The Economists, and American Economic Policy, 1921–1933* (1985); and John Garraty, *The Great Depression* (1986), ought to be consulted also.

On Hoover's presidency there are the works of Harris Gaylord Warren, *Herbert Hoover and the Great Depression* (1959); J. Joseph Huthmacher and Warren I. Susman, eds. *Herbert Hoover and the Crisis of American Capitalism* (1973); Wilson, *Herbert Hoover;* and David Burner, *Herbert Hoover* (1978). Schlesinger explores Hoover "revisionism" in "Hoover Makes A Comeback," *New York Review of Books* March 8, 1979.

The liberal historians who have written important books on Roosevelt and the New Deal have been crucial in establishing conventional views of American politics. The most distinguished are James McGregor Burns, *Roosevelt: The Lion and the Fox* (1956) as well as his *The Deadlock of Democracy* (1963); Schlesinger, *The Age of Roosevelt*, 3 vols. to date (1956–1960) and also his *The Imperial Presidency* (1973); Frank Freidel, *Franklin D. Roosevelt*, 4 vols. to date (1952–1973); Leuchtenburg, *The Perils of Prosperity, 1914–1932* (1958) and *Franklin D. Roosevelt*. Also important is Leuchtenburg's *A Troubled Feast* (1973, 1986). A more recent survey of the thirties is Robert McElvaine's *The Great Depression, 1929–1939* (1984); the latest biography is Kenneth S. Davis's, *FDR: The New Deal Years*, 1933–1937 (1986).

McElvaine's editing of *Down and Out in the Great Depression: Letters from the Forgotten Man* (1983) as well as Studs Terkel, *Hard Times* (1970), and Ann Banks, *First Person America* (1980) are good places to begin to get a flavor of the people's sense of politics under Roosevelt.

A manuscript by Samuel P. Hays, "The New Deal: After Fifty Years" (University of Pittsburgh, xerox, 1985) contains an extensive bibliography of monographic literature on the New Deal. A number of these monographs on the politics of the thirties reveal the complexities of evaluation: Ellis Hawley, *The New Deal and the Problem of Monopoly* (1966); Robert F. Himmelberg, *The Origins of the National Recovery Administration: Business, Government, and the Trade Association Issue, 1921–1933* (1976); Eliot A. Rosen, *Hoover, Roosevelt, and the Brains Trust* (1977); James E. Sargent, *Roosevelt and the Hundred Days* (1981); Alfred U. Romasco, *The Politics of Recovery* (1983); and Mark H. Leff, *The Limits of Symbolic Reform: The New Deal and Taxation, 1933–1939* (1984). Also of interest are Leff's "Taxing the Forgotten Man: The Politics of Social Security Finance in the New Deal," *Journal of American History* 70 (1983); Bradford A. Lee's work on economic problems of the New Deal—for a sample see his "The New Deal Reconsidered," *Wilson Quarterly* 6 (1982); and the essays of Theda Skocpol, for example, "Political Response to Capitalist Crisis: Neo-Marxist Theories of the State and the Case of the New Deal," *Politics and Society* 10 (1980) and, with Kenneth Finegold, "State Capacity and Economic Intervention in the Early New Deal," *Political Science Quarterly*, 97 (Summer 1982).

For Roosevelt's image, see William McKinley Moore's "FDR's Image—A Study in Pictorial Symbols," Ph.D. dissertation, University of Wisconsin, 1946. For Roosevelt's sense of his new politics, see Anne O'Hare McCormick, "As He Sees Himself," *New York Times Magazine*, October 16, 1938, and Leo Ribuffo, *The Old Christian Right* (1983). On his paralysis, see Hugh Gregory Gallagher, *FDR's Splendid Deception* (1985). Bruce Russett's *No Clear and Present Danger* (1972) suggests the problems of "would have" analysis in understanding American foreign policy during the war.

On welfare and planning, see Thomas K. McCraw, *Prophets of Regulation* (1985); James T. Patterson, *America's Struggle Against Poverty, 1900–1980* (1981); Howell John Harris, *The Right to Manage: Industrial Relations Policies of American Business in the 1940s* (1982); and Charles Murray, *Losing Ground: American Social Policy, 1950–1980* (1984).

2. HOOVER, ROOSEVELT, AND THE GREAT
DEPRESSION
The contribution of Gerald D. Nash to Joseph Huthmacher and Warren Susman, *Herbert Hoover and the Crisis of American Capitalism* compares the careful presentation of self by both Hoover and Nixon. William Leuchtenburg's recollection of Roosevelt's vitality comes in a letter to me of 24 March 1985.

3. LESSONS OF THE MASTER
Bernard Bellush wrote of the NRA's "dismal failure" in *The Failure of the NRA* (1975), and Otis Graham in *Toward A Planned Society* wrote of the need for a "fair trial." John T. Flynn in *The Roosevelt Myth* (1948) wrote of FDR's smashing and battering (I have altered his text from "smashing" to "smashed"); Frances Fox and Richard Cloward authored *Regulating the Poor* (1971). The contrasting favorable estimate of the New Deal comes from Bernard Bailyn, et al., *Great Republic* (2nd. ed).

4. ROOSEVELT AND THE STRUCTURE OF POLITICS

Arthur Schlesinger is quoted from his *The Age of Roosevelt: The Politics of Upheaval* (1960); Frank Freidel from his *Franklin D. Roosevelt: Launching the New Deal* (1973); Robert McElvaine from his *Great Depression;* Alonzo Hamby from one of his introductions to an anthology he edited, *The New Deal,* 2nd. ed. (1981); Gabriel Kolko from his *Wealth and Power in America* (1962); William Appleman Williams from his *The Contours of American History* (1966); William G. Dumhoff from his *The Higher Circles* (1970); James Patterson from "The New Deal and the States," *American Historical Review* 73 (October 1967); and Edgar Eugene Robinson from *The Roosevelt Leadership, 1933–1945* (1955).

For various evaluations of Truman, see Barton J. Bernstein, ed., *Politics and Policies of the Truman Administration* (1970); Alonzo Hamby, *Beyond the New Deal: Harry S. Truman and American Liberalism* (1973); Hamby, ed., *Harry S. Truman and the Fair Deal* (1974); Richard S. Kirkendall, ed., *The Truman Period as a Research Field: A Reappraisal* (1972); and Robert Ferrell, *Harry S. Truman.*

Donald R. McCoy, *The Presidency of Harry Truman* (1984) is a mine of information on Truman's character. Garry Wills's "Truman" in *Lead Time* (1984) is angry but astute, as are many of his characterizations in the book. Even more astute are Godfrey Hodgson, "Puritan from the Poker Room, *New Republic,* 195, 8 (1986) and Robert Griffith, "Harry S Truman and the Burden of Modernity," *Reviews in American History* 9 (1981). Many of the essays in *Harry S. Truman: The Man from Independence,* ed. William F. Levantrosser (1986) ought also to be examined. Important to some of the points I have made about the Truman administration are Aaron Wildavsky. *Dixon-Yates* (1962); David A. Frier, *Conflict of Interest in the Eisenhower Administration* (1969); Maeva Marcus, *Truman and the Steel Seizure Case* (1977); Robert H. Ferrell, ed. *Off the Record: The Private Papers of Harry S. Truman* (1981); Robert Underhill, *The Truman Persuasions* (1981); Monte M. Poen, ed. *Strictly Personal and Confidential: The Letters Harry Truman Never Mailed* (1981); Andrew Dunbar, *The Truman Scandals and the Politics of Morality* (1984); and Margaret Truman, *Bess W. Truman* (1986).

On the connected issues of anticommunism at home and abroad I have relied on different literatures. On public opinion, see H. Schuyler Foster, *Activism Replaces Isolationism: U.S. Public Attitudes, 1940–1975* (1984). Richard Freeland, *Truman Doctrine* and John Earl Haynes, *Dubious Alliance: The Making of Minnesota's DFL Party* (1984) are perceptive. On the Marshall Plan and American economic policy, see Hadley Arkes, *Bureaucracy, The Marshall Plan, and the National Interest* (1973); Immanuel Wexler, *The Marshall Plan Revisited* (1983); Alan S. Milward, *The Reconstruction of Western Europe, 1945–1951* (1984); Robert A. Pollard, *Economic Security and the Origins of the Cold War, 1945–1950* (1985); and Michael J. Hogan, "American Marshall Planners and the Search for a European Neocapitalism," *American Historical Review*, 90 (1985). On McCarthyism, see Robert Griffith, *The Politics of Fear: Joseph R. McCarthy and the Senate* (1970); Richard M. Fried, *Men Against McCarthy* (1976); Peter L. Steinberg, *The Great "Red Menace"* (1984); and Richard H. Pells, *The Liberal Mind in a Conservative Age* (1985). Allen Weinstein's *Perjury: The Hiss-Chambers Case* (1978) is essential both for what it says about anticommunism in the thirties, forties, and fifties and about the climate of the late seventies when it was written. Rosemary Foot's *The Wrong War* (1984) contains an excellent survey on the various components that went into the decisions taken over Korea in 1950 and 1951. For recent accounts, see Burton I. Kaufman, *The Korean War* (1986), and William Stueck, "The Korean War as International History," *Diplomatic History*, 10 (1986).

### 5. A Problem of Authority

The frustrated voter quoted on Truman was my father; the young person was Murray G. Murphey—both in conversations with me. Robert Ferrell in *Harry S. Truman* notes that Truman was undervalued by contemporaries; Frederick Siegal in *Troubled Journey* makes the comment about Truman's entering a "hall of mirrors."

The liberal quotation is from Foster Rhea Dulles, *America's Rise to World Power, 1898–1954* (1954); the left, from Joyce and Gabriel Kolko, *The Limits of Power* (1972); the right, from Alvin J. Cottrell and James E. Dougherty, "The Lessons of Korea: War and the Power of Man," *Orbis*, 2 (Spring 1958). Theodore Lowi compares the steel seizure case to the Watergate scandals in *The Personal Presidency* (1985), and Maeva Marcus has written about

the precedents in *Truman and the Steel Seizure Case.* Athan Theo-
haris is quoted from "The Escalation of the Loyalty Program," in
Barton Berstein, *Politics and Policies of the Truman Administration;*
Richard Freeland from *The Truman Doctrine;* Joseph
Huthmacher from his "Introduction" to his edited collection of
essays *The Truman Years* (1972); Earl Latham is quoted in
Freeland; and Alonzo Hamby from his "Introduction" to his ed-
ited collection *Harry S. Truman and the Fair Deal.*

Drew McCoy in *The Presidency of Harry Truman* uses the
phrase "national scapegoat."

On Eisenhower, the most interesting appraisals are given in
Marquis Childs, *Eisenhower: Captive Hero* (1958); Herbert Parmet,
*Eisenhower and the American Crusades* (1973); Robert Divine, *Eisen-
hower and the Cold War* (1981); Fred Greenstein, *The Hidden-Hand
Presidency* (1982); Robert Griffith, "Dwight D. Eisenhower and
the Corporate Commonwealth," *American Historical Review* 87
(1982); Stephen Ambrose, *Eisenhower,* 2 vols. (1983, 1984);
Henry William Brands, Jr., *A Moment of Certainty: The Eisenhower
Administration and the Cold War* (manuscript, 1985); Robert F.
Burk, *Dwight D. Eisenhower: Hero & Politician* (1986); and Richard
A. Melanson and David Mayers, eds. *Reevaluating Eisenhower:
American Foreign Policy in the Fifties* (1987).

The literature on Kennedy is enormous, and an excellent
book that blends scholarship with more popular mythmaking is
Doris Kearns Goodwin, *The Fitzgeralds and the Kennedys* (1987),
as is David Burner and Thomas R. West, *The Torch is Passed: The
Kennedy Brothers and American Liberalism* (1984). On the president
himself, see Herbert Parmet, *Jack* (1980); and *JFK* (1983). Arthur Schlesinger, Jr., *A Thousand Days* (1965), is still a valuable
document.

### 6 AND 7. MOMENT OF CERTAINTY

Blanche Wiesen Cook is quoted from her *The Declassified
Eisenhower: A Divided Legacy of Peace and Political Warfare* (1981),
where William Shannon and Eric Goldman are also quoted; Howard Zinn from his *Postwar America, 1945–1971* (1973); all the
Fred Greenstein citations are from *Hidden-Hand Presidency.* David
A. Frier in *Conflict of Interest in the Eisenhower Administration* writes
that the Republican scandals were as serious as Truman's, and

Alonzo Hamby states that Eisenhower could not be defeated in 1960 in *Liberalism and Its Challengers*.

The line "More than a president is dead . . . " comes from Arnold Greenberg, "November 22, 1963" in *A Patch of Grass* (1964). Forrest McDonald argues that Kennedy was as bad as Taft in dealing with Congress in his *The United States in the Twentieth Century* (1970). The quotations about the Kennedy family can be found on the relevant dates (e.g., November 23, 1983) in the *New York Times*.

Jim Heath wrote *Decade of Disillusionment: The Kennedy-Johnson Years* (1975); William Chafe talks about the arguments of Kennedy's supporters in *Unfinished Journey;* Frederick Siegal is quoted from *Troubled Journey;* Richard Walton from *Cold War and Counter-Revolution: The Foreign Policy of John F. Kennedy* (1972); Bruce Miroff from *Pragmatic Illusions: The Presidential Politics of John F. Kennedy* (1976); Herbert Parmet from *JFK;* and Dewey Grantham from *Recent America* (1987).

On civil rights, see, among others, Harvard Sitkoff *The Struggle for Black Equality* (1983) and Charles and Barbara Whalen, *The Longest Debate: A Legislative History of the 1964 Civil Rights Act* (1986); Jack Bloom, *Class, Race, and the Civil Rights Movement* (1987). On the sixties, see: Townsend Hoopes, *The Limits of Intervention* (1973); Allen Matusow, *The Unraveling of America* (1984); Schlesinger's *Robert Kennedy and His Times* (1978); Michael X. Delli Carpini, *Stability and Change in American Politics: The Coming of Age of the Generation of the 1960s* (1986); and John Hellman, *American Myth and the Legacy of Vietnam* (1986).

For Johnson, provocative interpretations are given by Doris Kearns, *Lyndon Johnson and the American Dream* (1976), some aspects of which I have heavily relied on; Robert A. Caro, *The Years of Lyndon Johnson: The Path to Power* (1982); Ronnie Dugger, *The Politician: The Life and Times of Lyndon Johnson—The Drive for Power, from the Frontier to Master of the Senate* (1984); Robert A. Divine, ed. *Exploring the Johnson Years* (1981); David Zarefsky, *President Johnson's War on Poverty* (1986); Paul K. Conkin, *Big Daddy from the Pedernales, Lyndon Baines Johnson* (1986).

### 8. "LET US REASON TOGETHER"
Vaughan Davis Bornet in *The Presidency of Lyndon Johnson* (1983) calls the sixties the era of the big promise. Thomas Bailey

and David Kennedy are quoted from *The American Pageant* (1983); Doris Kearns from *Lyndon Johnson and the American Dream;* Gunther Lewy from *America in Vietnam* (1978) (where the verb phrase I use, "would have prevented," appears as "would prevent"); and William Appleman Williams from *Empire as a Way of Life* (1980).

On Nixon, must reading is his *Six Crises* (1962). Gary Wills is again astute in *Nixon Agonistes* (1969). More conventional and outraged is Jonathan Schell, *Time of Illusion* (1976). Of the memoirs of Watergate I have found the most useful to be John W. Dean, III, *Blind Ambition* (1976) and H. R. Haldeman, *The Ends of Power* (1978).

### 9. Nixon and the Watergate Scandal

Andrew Dunbar, in the *Truman Scandals and the Politics of Morality* writes of the "dirty tricks department" under Truman.

The liberal view is from Arthur S. Link, William A. Link, and William B. Catton, *American Epoch,* 6th ed. (1987); the left view from Norman L. Rosenberg and Emily S. Rosenberg, *In Our Time,* 2nd. ed. (1982). I have constructed the conservative view from conversations with conservative historians; I have not been able to find one in print.

### Conclusion:

Ronald Radosh is quoted from "The Myth of the New Deal," in Radosh and Murray Rothbard, eds., *A New History of Leviathan: Essays on the Rise of the American Corporate State* (1972); Paul Conkin from *The New Deal;* Carl Degler from *Out of Our Past* (1959, 1970).

Behan Mccullagh's *Justifying Historical Descriptions* (1985) contains a bibliography of philosophical works on the problem of "counterfactual conditionals," the problem that, I have argued, stumps history. The most recent treatment is Murray G. Murphey, "Explanation, Causes, and Covering Laws," *History and Theory, Beiheft,* 25 (1986). The seminal work, however, Nelson Goodman's *Fact, Fiction, and Forecast* (1955 and more recent editions), should be mentioned separately.

Other works of a theoretical or methodological nature have shaped my concerns: Jonathan Edwards, *Religious Affections* (1746); Edward D. Griffin, *The Doctrine of Divine Efficiency* (1833); Friedrich Nietzsche, *The Use and Abuse of History* (1874); Max Scheler, *Ressentiment* (1912); Georges Sorel, *Reflections on Violence* (1908); George Santayana, *Skepticism and Animal Faith* (1923); Harold D. Lasswell, *Psychopathology and Politics* (1930); Ernst Bloch, *Das Prinzip Hoffnung*, 3 vols. (1954–59); Charles L. Stevenson, *Facts and Values* (1963); Bernard Bailyn, *The Ideological Origins of the American Revolution* (1967); Robert William Fogel, *Railroads and American Economic Growth* (1964); Paul Kleppner, *The Cross of Culture: A Social Analysis of Midwestern Politics, 1850–1900* (1970); Robert Ackerman, "Frazer on Myth and Ritual," *Journal of the History of Ideas* (1975); Sacvan Bercovitch, *The American Jeremiad* (1978); R. M. Hare, *Moral Reasoning* (1981); and Michael E. McGerr, *The Decline of Popular Politics: The American North 1865–1928* (1986).

Some of my own essays deal with similar methodological problems: "The Mind of the Historian," *History and Theory* 8 (1969); "History as a Way of Learning," *American Quarterly* 22 (1970); Review of J. H. Hexter, *The History Primer, History and Theory* 11 (1972); "Myth and Symbol in American Studies," *American Quarterly* 24 (1972); and "John Dewey, American Theology, and Scientific Politics" (forthcoming).

# ★ Index